Low Fat

The best recipes
for low-fat cooking

DUMONT
monte

Low Fat

The best recipes
for low-fat cooking

Sandra Schäffer

Photographs by Brigitte Sporrer
and Alena Hrbkova

General hints

Eggs: If not otherwise stated, the eggs used in these recipes are of medium size.

Milk: If not otherwise stated, milk used in these recipes is whole milk (3.5% fat content).

Poultry: Poultry should always be cooked right through before eating. You can tell if it is done by piercing it with a skewer. If the juices run out pink, then it is not ready and must be cooked for a longer time. If the juices are clear then the bird is done.

Nuts: Some of these recipes contain nuts or nut oil. People who have allergies or who tend to be allergic should avoid eating these dishes.

Herbs: If not otherwise stated, these recipes call for fresh herbs. If you cannot obtain these, the amounts in the recipes can be replaced with half the quantity of dried herbs.

The temperatures and times in these recipes are based on using a conventional oven. If you are using a fan oven, please follow the manufacturer's instructions .

Contents

Low fat – a short-lived trend or an increasingly serious approach to eating?

Cholesterol, the cause of many illnesses

Eating is an essential need of every living being, but not everything that people eat contributes to their health. The science of modern dietetics has discovered that many illnesses of the civilized world, including in particular heart disease and circulation problems, are caused by excessive consumption of fat as well as by stress, lack of exercise and smoking.

An excessive level of cholesterol in the blood contributes to blocked arteries and in turn increases the risk of heart infarction. Excessive cholesterol is caused by saturated fatty acids, which are present in meat and sausages and also in dairy products such as butter, cream and eggs.

However, giving up fat altogether is not recommended, because as well as all the essential nutrients, the body needs the beneficial unsaturated fatty acids in order to function properly. Butter and cream contain these unsaturated fatty acids as well as the damaging saturated ones.

The optimum energy balance

To ensure an optimum energy balance, it is essential to eat a healthy diet. This means being aware of the various vitamins, minerals and trace elements that are present in each individual food. The amount of fat in an individual's daily diet should not exceed 30% of the daily intake of energy. Depending on the overall energy intake, this is equivalent to between 60 g/2 oz and 90 g/3 oz a day. But in Europe the average fat intake per person is actually 130 g/4½ oz per day!

By following the essential ground rules of modern dietetics, the consumption of fat will automatically go down. Besides the obvious health aspects, this has the important advantage that the problems of excess weight and subcutaneous fat will gradually disappear automatically. A well-balanced diet is also the prerequisite for feeling well in oneself.

A healthy lifestyle need not mean privation

A low-fat diet does not mean giving up good food. On the contrary, low-fat dishes can be very delicious, as is shown by the recipes in this book. The various sections – Breakfast, Snacks, Main Dishes, Desserts and Drinks – will enable you to plan and vary your meals every day according to your own personal taste. The indications of fat

content and calories that accompany each recipe will help you control your intake of fat. So, for instance, on a day when you have a fairly rich lunch, you can plan an evening meal that is particularly light

Low-fat cooking

A low-fat diet does not imply a strictly vegetarian health diet or a plain, boring food regime. Above all it means making a deliberate, careful choice and combination of foods which will provide you with all the vital nutrients. Many of the recipes in this book are inspired by Mediterranean and Oriental cuisine which have all the essentials for a light, healthy diet: plenty of fresh vegetables, aromatic herbs and spices, unsaturated fatty acids in the form of cold-pressed vegetable oils, and fairly small amounts of lean meat and fish.

Which nutrients does the body need?

In order to feel healthy and well, the body needs particular nutrients. The organism can only function properly if the composition of the various substances is well-balanced and consistent. An unbalanced diet will not have consequences that are apparent at once, but in the long term it will damage the body. Indeed, a diet containing too much fat and too few vitamins and minerals can result in excessive weight gain and a depressed immune system.

Body weight as an indicator

The best indicator of a balanced diet is body weight. If your calorie intake is too high, your weight goes up! However, the ideal calorie intake is not the same for everyone. People burn up calories and fat at different rates. In addition, the burning of calories also depends on your physical and sporting activity. Those who practise sport and whose work involves hard physical labour burn up more calories and can therefore eat more without putting on weight. But the amount of fat in the calorie intake should still be controlled, because the body tends to store fat. If your calorie intake is well-balanced, your body weight will be too.

The ideal ratio of nutrients

Carbohydrates
The largest part of a balanced diet should consist of carbohydrates, which should represent 55–60% of the food intake. Carbohydrates are present in potatoes, pasta, vegetables, rice and bread. These foods also provide a lot of fibre which is important for the digestion and metabolism. These foods are only fattening in combination with fat, so a larger amount can be eaten without fat! Instead of serving pasta with a cream-based sauce, serve it with a light tomato sauce, and instead of baked potato with mayonnaise, enjoy it with herb-flavoured quark.

and must absorb these substances through food. Animal proteins are present in dairy products, eggs, fish and lean meat. But it is important that these dairy products should not contain too much fat, but plenty of healthy lactic acids. These are present in high levels in low-fat quark, low-fat milk and low-fat yoghurt kefir. Vegetable proteins are found in pulses, potatoes, vegetables, wholemeal (wholewheat) products and nuts. In order to ensure that the body has all the kinds of proteins it needs, it is important to eat a diet with a balanced source of proteins, two-thirds of which should be derived from vegetable sources. For instance, an ideal combination would be a baked potato with low-fat quark or wholemeal (wholewheat) bread with cottage cheese.

Protein

The second most important nutrient in our diet is protein which should represent about 15% of the daily food intake. This corresponds to between 45 and 55 g (about 1½–2 oz) per day. Proteins are made up of various components known as amino acids. Amino acids are involved in the building of cells, endogenous enzymes and hormones. The body's metabolism dismantles the proteins contained in food and converts it into endogenous protein. The body is unable to produce the most important proteins, namely the essential amino acids,

Fats

The third component in the daily diet is fat, which should represent between 25–30% of the daily calorie intake, namely 60 to 90 g (2–3 oz) per day. Fats are a source of energy and contain fat-soluble vitamins. For instance, vitamins A, D, E and K cannot be absorbed by the body without fat. The important thing is to choose the right kind of fat. Fats are divided into saturated, unsaturated and poly-unsaturated fats. The body can produce the first two types of fat so that it is only necessary to worry about providing the body with sufficient polyunsaturated fatty acids. But many people eat too much of the wrong kind of fat, the saturated fats which are present in fatty meat and sausages, full-cream dairy products, chocolate, cakes and pastries. Saturated fatty acids cause a rise in cholesterol levels in the blood and, combined with a lack of exercise, they increase the danger of heart infarction and strokes.

The amount of polyunsaturated fatty acids is often too low. A low-fat diet usually means reducing the intake of fat, and the

fat that is consumed should be polyunsaturated fatty acids. These are present in vegetable oils such as cold-pressed olive oil, thistle oil, sunflower oil, fish, cereals, avocados and nuts. The daily amount of polyunsaturated fatty acid needed by the body is only 1½ tablespoons of vegetable oil.

Vitamins and minerals
Minerals and vitamins contribute greatly to our general physical well-being – they ensure the smooth functioning of all the

Preparation methods in low-fat cooking

Low-fat cuisine does not just mean choosing the right ingredients: it also requires the right cooking methods. For instance, it makes no sense to braise fresh vegetables longer than necessary or to cook them in a large amount of water which will be poured away after cooking, together with the important vitamins and minerals contained in the cooking liquid. Nor is it sensible to use butter, lard or coconut oil for frying meat and fish, and the sauces made to accompany vegetable and meat dishes should not always be made with cream or crème fraîche. But this does not mean that you should give up all your favourite dishes or that the food should taste any less good. All that is required is to use different, healthier cooking methods instead of the traditional methods such as lengthy boiling or frying in a lot of fat.

important processes in our body. However, alcohol and coffee counteract the beneficial effect of vitamins, as do stress and smoking. Even if you eat a well-balanced diet with plenty of fresh fruit and vegetables, cereals and dairy products, it is advisable to back this up with vitamins and minerals.

Steaming

For this you will need an ordinary saucepan, preferably stainless steel, a steamer basket and a tightly fitting lid. The steamer basket may take the form of a stainless steel colander with slats which can be made larger or smaller, according to the size of the saucepan. Chinese bamboo steamers which are simply placed in the saucepan are also suitable. Steaming is a very simple

cooking method. The saucepan is filled with a small amount of water or stock (broth) – little enough for the vegetables not to come into contact with the water. The steamer basket is then placed in the saucepan with the vegetables, meat or fish in it. The lid should fit fairly closely so that the liquid evaporates as little as possible during the steaming process. The liquid should be brought to the boil very quickly and then reduced to a medium heat. It is important to check with a fork or sharp, pointed knife to see if the food is cooked because the cooking time for different vegetables varies enormously. For instance, fennel takes twice as long to cook as courgettes. Steamed vegetables maintain their natural colour and taste much better than boiled ones. They are delicious served with a sprinkling of fresh herbs and a little pepper or lemon juice.

Braising

Vegetables and meat are also delicious when braised. This process means cooking in a covered saucepan with a small amount of liquid, or none at all, and very little fat, using a medium heat. Vegetables contain a lot of water, which is why it is usually unnecessary for any more to be added. Braising too is a very healthy way of cooking food since it does not destroy the important vitamins and minerals present in meat or vegetables.

Stir-frying

This method of cooking requires a wok which is a Chinese frying pan. Stir-frying is a very easy and extremely healthy way of cooking. But it is important that all the ingredients should be chopped small in advance. This reduces the cooking time so that the vegetables remain crispy and retain their "bite". Low-fat meat or fish, cut into strips, are also ideal for wok cooking.

This is how to cook in a wok. Heat a very small amount of olive oil or ground nut oil

in the wok. Add the vegetables, fish and meat cut into small pieces, and fry over a high heat, stirring constantly, for 3 to 5 minutes, so as to preserve the flavour and vitamin content.

Flavouring with herbs and spices

Herbs and spices play an important part in low-fat cuisine. They can enhance the flavour of vegetables and lean meat and add a surprising dimension to a dish. By definition, low-fat cooking precludes the addition of fat which is a taste conductor and gives food its particular aroma. This is why the addition of fresh aromatic herbs is so important. In addition, many fresh herbs, such as parsley, are full of vitamin C. Almost every savoury dish will benefit from the addition of chives, cress, lemon balm, coriander, tarragon, basil, dill or chervil. Low-fat cooking also depends heavily on spices such as peppercorns, which add an interesting spicy aroma when freshly ground, paprika, nutmeg, dried herbes de Provence, and last but not least various oriental spices such as turmeric.

Salt, however, should be used sparingly because the body does not need it in large amounts. Salt is already present in quite large quantities in ready-made foods such as bread and cheese. Lemon juice makes an excellent substitute and it is ideal for seasoning vegetable dishes, braised meat or fish and in salad dressings. Finely chopped fresh ginger, grated horseradish, garlic, chillies and lemon grass are also extremely useful in low-fat cuisine because they add a refined, sophisticated flavour to a wide range of dishes.

The pleasure of puddings without guilt

The high levels of sugar and fat present in puddings and cakes are particularly bad for your health. Unrefined white sugar does not contain any important nutrients but only "empty" calories which are soon converted into fat by the body. Nevertheless, there is no need to do without puddings and cakes in low-fat cuisine. Calorie-reduced puddings made with fresh fruit, low-fat dairy products and cereals can be sweetened with honey or maple syrup. A little vanilla sugar, cinnamon

and grated orange or lemon zest will add a delicious aroma to any pudding.

What should you buy?

So when you go shopping, what should you buy and what should you avoid in order to eat healthily?

Basically, you should always buy fresh food and choose products which have not been polluted with harmful chemicals and which have not been processed.

Recommended items include the following:

- Fish
- Butter in small quantities, vegetable oils – cold-pressed if possible – such as olive oil, sunflower oil, thistle and pumpkin seed oil
- Nuts in small amounts
- Mineral water, herb teas, fruit juices and vegetable juices

... and what should you avoid?

What kind of foods are best suited to a healthy, calorie-reduced diet?

In principle, the most important aspect of low-fat cuisine should be the pleasure of eating. When you discover the delights of crisp vegetable salads, you will hardly miss the heavy, fatty meals of the past. When buying food products, check the details on the packet or tin, where the contents will be listed. But be cautious, because many ready-made or processed foods contain hidden fat of which one is not aware. You should buy the following products as little as possible:

- Ready-made dishes such as canned food, canned or packet soups, frozen meals
- Pork, fatty poultry such as goose and duck
- Sausages with a high fat content such as salami, liver sausage and so on
- Full-fat cheeses such as processed cheese, Camembert, Gouda
- Dairy products with a high fat content such as cream and condensed milk

- Seasonal vegetables, fresh if possible
- Fruit
- Pulses
- Grains such as wholemeal (wholewheat) bread, cereals, pasta and rice
- Dairy products (especially with lactic acid bacteria) such as yoghurt, kefir and quark. But note: it is essential to choose the low-calorie versions!
- Eggs, but no more than 2 or 3 a week because of their high cholesterol levels.
- Lean meat and sausages (beef, lamb or poultry)

- Mayonnaise, margarine and clarified butter
- Chocolate, cakes and pastries containing cream, butter-cream, cream-based puddings and ice cream
- Snacks with a high fat content such as potato chips and peanuts
- Alcoholic drinks

Indispensable kitchen utensils

Vegetables and fruit play an important part in low-fat cuisine. If possible you should eat vegetables and fruit every day because of all the vitamins and minerals they contain. However, these nutrients are easily destroyed if the food is not prepared and cooked properly. It is important to observe the following guidelines and to be equipped with the necessary kitchen utensils.

For cleaning carrots and potatoes, it is helpful to have a brush so that you can scrub the vegetables under the tap (faucet), thus removing all trace of earth without peeling. When peeling fruit and vegetables, try and removing as little skin as possible because all the most important nutrients are situated just under the skin. A potato peeler will help you peel potatoes and apples as thinly as possible.

An adjustable mandoline or vegetable slicer will also be very useful in preparing vegetables and fruit because it makes it easy

to cut the food into strips or slices of the right thickness as required. For herbs, you will need a good chopping knife or sharp kitchen scissors.

A juicer makes it simple to prepare fruit and vegetables juices, while a food processor can save a lot of hand work in preparing fruit and vegetables.

A hand-held mixer which can purée cooked fruit and vegetables in a few seconds is invaluable for making soups and sauces. The appliance is easily cleaned under hot running water.

A non-stick pan with a glass lid is also recommended. This will enable you to cook vegetables and meat without any fat, and the glass lid makes it easy to check the progress of the food. A wok is invaluable for stir-frying vegetables, seafood and meat. With woks there is a choice between ordinary steel and stainless steel. If the wok is to be used on an electric hob, choose a one with a flat base. Use a wooden or stainless steel spatula to stir the meat, fish or vegetables while frying.

For braising and stewing you will need one or two stainless steel saucepans with closely fitting lids. The bottom of the pan must be a good conductor of heat so that the food can be braised quickly.

For steaming, which is a particularly healthy way of cooking, you will need an extendable metal steamer basket or a Chinese steamer basket.

Last but not least you will need a balloon whisk, a small but indispensable utensil in the kitchen.

Quantity per 100 g	Energy (kcal)	Protein (g)	Fat (g)	Carbohydrate (g)	Cholesterol (mg)	Magnesium (mg)	Calcium (mg)	Iron (mg)	Vitamin A (µg)	Vitamin E (mg)	Vitamin C (mg)
Squid, cooked	95,0	18,42	1,2	2,4	150,0	37,0	48,0	2,2	6,0	2,3	2,5
Eel, cooked	266,7	18,0	21,9	0,0	181,0	22,0	22,0	0,6	812,0	9,2	1,4
Angler fish, cooked	74,2	14,9	1,5	0,0	25,0	30,0	20,0	0,3	7,0	1,0	1,0
Mackerel, cooked	210,3	21,5	13,9	0,0	87,0	31,0	14,0	1,0	61,0	1,7	0,3
Tuna fish, in oil	347,6	17,3	31,3	0,0	55,0	29,0	28,0	0,8	248,0	13,2	0,5
Salmon	130,9	18,4	6,3	0,0	35,0	29,0	13,0	1,0	41,0	2,2	0,0
Low-fat beef, cooked	151,2	28,9	3,8	0,0	73,0	21,0	7,0	3,1	24,0	0,6	0,0
Low-fat veal, cooked	152,6	27,2	4,8	0,0	74,0	23,0	27,0	2,0	1,0	0,3	0,0
Low-fat pork	135,9	21,2	5,6	0,0	70,0	25,0	2,0	1,1	6,0	0,4	0,0
Chicken breast	101,9	23,5	0,7	0,0	66,0	27,0	14,0	0,5	27,0	0,3	0,0
Turkey breast	106,7	24,1	1,0	0,0	60,0	20,0	13,0	1,0	1,0	0,9	0,0
Parsley	52,6	4,4	0,4	7,4	0,0	41,0	245,0	5,5	902,0	3,7	166,0
Chives	27,3	3,6	0,6	1,6	0,0	44,0	129,0	1,9	50,0	1,6	47,0
Watercress	18,7	1,6	0,3	2,0	0,0	34,0	180,0	3,1	692,0	1,0	51,0
Lamb's lettuce	14,4	1,8	0,4	0,7	0,0	13,0	35,0	2,0	650,0	0,6	35,0
Head lettuce	11,7	1,3	0,2	1,1	0,0	11,0	37,0	1,0	240,0	0,6	13,0
Leaf spinach, cooked	16,0	2,3	0,3	0,4	0,0	36,0	123,0	3,2	723,0	1,4	24,1
Celery	16,7	1,2	0,2	2,2	0,0	12,0	80,0	0,5	483,0	0,2	7,0
Broccoli	23,2	3,2	0,2	1,9	0,0	23,0	112,0	1,2	137,0	0,7	61,1
Fennel	24,6	2,4	0,3	2,8	0,0	49,0	109,0	2,7	783,0	6,0	93,0
Asparagus	14,6	1,7	0,1	1,4	0,0	11,0	25,0	0,5	79,0	2,0	9,0
Leek	23,0	2,3	0,3	2,5	0,0	12,0	93,0	0,8	168,0	0,6	12,1
Aubergine (eggplant)	17,5	1,2	0,2	2,5	0,0	11,0	13,0	0,4	7,0	0,0	2,8
Pea	81,8	6,6	0,5	12,3	0,0	33,0	24,0	1,8	72,0	0,3	25,0
Beans	25,4	2,4	0,2	3,2	0,0	25,0	63,0	0,8	56,0	0,1	12,2
Courgette (zucchini)	19,1	1,6	0,4	2,0	0,0	22,0	30,0	1,5	58,0	0,5	16,0
Carrots	25,8	1,0	0,2	4,8	0,0	18,0	41,0	2,11	574,0	0,5	7,0
Cucumber	12,2	0,6	0,2	1,8	0,0	8,0	15,0	0,5	66,0	0,1	8,0
Potato	70,3	2,0	0,1	14,6	0,0	19,0	6,0	0,4	1,0	0,1	12,3
Tomato	19,6	1,1	0,2	2,9	0,0	15,0	16,0	0,5	94,0	1,0	15,2

Quantity per 100 g	Energy (kcal)	Protein (g)	Fat (g)	Carbohydrate (g)	Cholesterol (mg)	Magnesium (mg)	Calcium (mg)	Iron (mg)	Vitamin A (µg)	Vitamin E (mg)	Vitamin C (mg)
Paprika	20,3	1,2	0,3	0,3	0,0	12,0	11,0	0,7	180,0	2,8	77,2
Onion	28,0	1,3	0,3	4,9	0,0	11,0	31,0	0,5	1,0	0,1	8,1
Garlic	141,9	6,1	0,1	28,4	0,0	35,0	38,0	1,4	0,0	0,0	14,0
Apple	51,9	0,3	0,4	11,4	0,0	6,0	7,0	0,5	8,0	0,5	12,0
Pear	52,4	0,5	0,3	12,4	0,0	7,0	9,0	0,3	3,0	0,4	5,0
Apricot	42,3	0,9	0,1	8,5	0,0	10,0	17,0	0,6	298,0	0,5	9,0
Nectarine	56,9	0,9	0,1	12,4	0,0	10,0	4,0	0,5	73,0	0,5	8,0
Peach	40,7	0,8	0,1	8,9	0,0	9,0	7,0	0,5	73,0	1,0	10,0
Strawberry	32,1	0,8	0,4	5,5	0,0	15,0	25,0	1,0	8,0	0,1	65,0
Raspberry	34,0	1,3	0,3	4,8	0,0	30,0	40,0	1,0	3,0	0,9	25,0
Grape	71,1	0,7	0,3	15,6	0,0	9,0	18,0	0,5	4,0	0,7	4,0
Pineapple	58,9	0,5	0,2	13,1	0,0	17,0	16,0	0,4	10,0	0,1	19,0
Banana	95,2	1,1	0,2	21,4	0,0	36,0	9,0	0,6	38,0	0,3	12,0
Walnut	655,0	14,4	62,5	10,6	0,0	130,0	87,0	2,5	8,0	6,0	2,6
Hazelnut (filbert)	636,8	12,0	61,6	10,5	0,0	155,0	225,0	3,8	5,0	26,3	3,0
Brazil nut	661,0	13,6	66,8	3,5	0,0	160,0	132,0	3,4	0,0	7,6	0,7
Almond	570,0	18,7	54,1	3,7	0,0	220,0	250,0	4,1	20,0	26,1	0,8
Low-fat milk	48,6	3,4	1,6	4,9	6,0	12,0	120,0	0,1	14,0	0,0	1,0
Kefir	49,8	3,4	1,5	4,1	6,0	12,0	120,0	0,1	22,0	0,0	1,0
Yoghurt (1%)	38,0	4,3	0,1	4,2	1,0	13,0	140,0	0,1	1,0	0,0	1,0
Parmesan	440,0	32,3	34,8	0,0	82,0	44,0	1200,0	0,6	415,0	1,0	0,0
Camembert	288,8	21,0	22,8	0,0	70,0	20,0	500,0	0,3	362,0	0,5	0,0
Sheep's cheese	236,8	17,0	18,8	0,0	45,0	25,0	450,0	0,6	228,0	0,5	0,0
Feta	236,8	17,0	18,8	0,0	45,0	25,0	450,0	0,6	228,0	0,5	0,0
Mozzarella	255,0	19,0	19,8	0,0	46,0	20,0	403,0	0,3	297,0	0,6	0,0
Olive oil	882,5	0,0	99,6	0,2	1,0	0,0	1,0	0,1	157,0	12,1	0,0
Vegetable oil	883,5	0,0	99,8	0,0	1,0	1,0	1,0	0,0	4,0	62,5	0,0
Sesame oil	881,6	0,2	99,5	0,0	1,0	0,0	10,0	0,1	0,0	3,5	0,0
Soya oil	872,7	0,0	98,6	0,0	2,0	0,0	0,0	0,0	583,0	17,0	0,0
Sunflower oil	883,5	0,0	99,8	0,0	1,0	1,0	1,0	0,0	4,0	62,5	0,0
Butter	741,9	0,7	83,2	0,6	240,0	3,0	13,0	0,1	653,0	2,0	0,2
Egg yolk	349,0	16,1	31,9	0,31	260,0	16,0	140,0	7,2	886,0	5,7	0,0
Egg white	49,8	11,1	0,2	0,7	0,0	12,0	11,0	0,2	0,0	0,0	0,3

Breakfast

Start the day with lots of energy and little fat, for instance, with a delicious Cinnamon muesli with raspberries (page 32) or a slice of tasty Crispbread with Parma ham (page 30). Breakfast should be something pleasant to wake up to. What about Bread with strawberries (page 50)? Whether sweet or savoury, a light, easily digestible breakfast is the most important meal of the day.

Wholemeal roll
with turkey

A delicious breakfast which is also an ideal snack for the office. Lean turkey breast is perfect for a low-calorie diet because it contains very little fat.

1 wholemeal roll

1 teaspoon diet margarine

2 slices lightly smoked
turkey breast

1 small carrot

4 radishes

salt

❶ Cut the wholemeal roll in half and spread diet margarine on both halves. Put a slice of turkey ham on each one.

❷ Peel the carrot and cut into thin slices. Wash and prepare the radishes, cut them in half, season with a little salt and arrange the sliced carrot and radish on each half roll.

Serves 1. About 120 kcal/500 kJ per serving.
Fat: 10 g • Carbohydrate: 23 g • Protein: 10 g

Crispbread with
Parma ham

A light, tasty breakfast which can also be accompanied by crudités if you like crisp, raw vegetables.

2 slices crispbread

2 tablespoons low-fat
fromage frais

4 thin slices Parma ham

a few leaves of basil

freshly ground pepper

1–2 small tomatoes

2–3 slices cucumber

❶ Spread fromage frais on 2 slices of wholemeal crispbread and put 2 slices of Parma ham on each one. Wash the basil leaves and dab dry. Garnish the crispbread topped with ham with the basil leaves and season with freshly ground pepper.

❷ Arrange the crispbread on a flat dish. Wash the tomatoes, remove the stalk and cut into slices. Arrange the tomato and cucumber slices around the two slices of crispbread.

Serves 1. About 140 kcal/580 kJ per serving.
Fat: 5 g • Carbohydrate: 7 g • Protein: 11 g

Three-grain muesli with sour milk

The various ingredients for this three-grain muesli are available in health food shops and in some supermarkets with a good health food section. You can also prepare a large amount of muesli in advance and store it in a jar with a screw-top lid where it will keep for up to four weeks.

❶ Place the wheat, spelt and barley in a large bowl and stir well. Add honey pops and raisins.

❷ Put the sunflower seeds in a non-stick pan and fry briefly without oil. Allow to cool down and add to the cereal mixture.

❸ Peel an apple, cut it in half and remove the core. Grate one apple half finely and add to the cereal mixture. Pour the sour milk over the cereal mixture, stir well and leave to stand for a few minutes. Garnish with the hazelnuts (filberts) before serving.

Serves 1. About 360 kcal/1510 kJ per serving.
Fat: 14 g • Carbohydrate: 38 g • Protein: 14 g

1 tablespoon wheat flakes

1 tablespoon spelt flakes

1 tablespoon barley flakes

1 tablespoon honey pops (puffed wheat, coated with honey)

1 teaspoon raisins

1 teaspoon sunflower seeds

½ apple

125 g/4½ oz sour milk

4–5 hazelnuts (filberts)

Cinnamon muesli
with raspberries

This delicious muesli is quick and easy to prepare. You can also use bilberries (blueberries) or blackberries instead of raspberries.

3 tablespoons oat flakes

2 pinches cinnamon

1 teaspoon maple syrup

1 tablespoon cornflakes

3 tablespoons low-fat quark

2 tablespoons low-fat milk
(1.5%)

1 teaspoon flaked (slivered)
almonds

1–2 tablespoons raspberries

❶ Put the oats, cinnamon and maple syrup in a deep bowl and stir well. Add the cornflakes and stir again.

❷ Pour the low-fat quark and milk into a small bowl, stir until smooth and pour over the cereal mixture. Sprinkle with almond flakes.

❸ Wash the raspberries, dab dry and garnish the muesli with them.

Serves 1. About 260 kcal/1090 kJ per serving.
Fat: 8 g • Carbohydrate: 32 g • Protein: 18 g

Fruit muesli

Fresh fruit muesli makes a delicious and healthy breakfast.
The fruit is full of vitamins and minerals, while the cereals provide
all the necessary energy needed by the body to start the day.

1 Chop the walnuts coarsely. Wash and prepare the berries. Peel the
bananas, wash and prepare the pears. Cut the fruit into bite-sized pieces,
put it all in a bowl and sprinkle with lemon juice.

2 Fry the spelt flakes briefly in a non-stick pan without any oil. Leave to cool
and pour them over the fruit.

3 Put the honey and cinnamon in a small bowl and stir well to obtain a
smooth mixture. Pour over the fruit and spelt flakes. Finally sprinkle the
coarsely chopped walnuts over the muesli, and leave to stand for a few
minutes.

Serves 1. About 415 kcal/1740 kJ per serving.
Fat: 23 g • Carbohydrate: 41 g • Protein: 11 g

1 tablespoon walnuts

1 tablespoon berries, for instance,
strawberries or blackberries

½ banana

½ pear

1 teaspoon lemon juice

3 tablespoons spelt flakes

1 small carton low-fat
yoghurt (1.5%)

1 pinch cinnamon

1 teaspoon honey

Crispbread with banana and bread with tomato

A sweet and savoury open sandwich, rich in nutrients and with very little fat. Instead of the banana, you could use peach slices.

1 slice crispbread

2 tablespoons cottage cheese

½ small banana

2–3 shelled hazelnuts (filberts)

a little honey (optional)

1 slice wholemeal (wholewheat) bread

1 tomato

3 sprigs parsley

salt

freshly ground pepper

❶ Spread 1 tablespoon cottage cheese on a slice of crispbread. Peel the banana, cut into slices and arrange on the crispbread with cottage cheese. Slice the hazelnuts (filberts) and place on the banana slices. Add the honey if desired.

❷ Spread the remaining cottage cheese on the slice of wholemeal bread. Wash the tomato, remove the stalk, cut into eight pieces and arrange on the bread. Wash the parsley, chop the leaves finely and sprinkle over the tomatoes. Season with a little salt and freshly ground pepper.

❸ Arrange the crispbread topped with banana and the wholemeal (wholewheat) bread with tomatoes on a large platter.

Serves 1. About 310 kcal/1300 kJ per serving.
Fat: 9 g • Carbohydrate: 43 g • Protein: 15 g

Fromage frais and apple open sandwich

A tasty sandwich for people who prefer a savoury breakfast: wholemeal bread with fromage frais will satisfy your hunger and set you up for the whole day.

❶ Spread the fromage frais on the slice of wholemeal bread and sprinkle a little paprika on top.

❷ Wash the cress and dab dry. Sprinkle the cress and sunflower seeds over the fromage frais.

❸ Wash the apple, cut into eight pieces and remove the core. Garnish the bread and fromage frais with the pieces of apple and arrange on a flat platter.

Serves 1. About 360 kcal/1510 kJ per serving.
Fat: 16 g • Carbohydrate: 39 g • Protein: 11 g

1 slice wholemeal (wholewheat) bread
20 g/¾ oz low-fat fromage frais
paprika
1 tablespoon cress
1 tablespoon sunflower seeds

Nectarine yoghurt

A fruity breakfast which is quick and easy to prepare. Instead of nectarine you can also use half a mango.

❶ Wash the nectarine carefully, pat dry, remove the stone (pit) and purée with a hand-mixer in a tall beaker. Stir in the yoghurt and sweeten with maple syrup.

❷ Fry the oat flakes in a non-stick frying pan without oil. Leave to cool briefly and stir into the yoghurt mixture. Put the nectarine yoghurt in a muesli bowl and sprinkle with almond flakes.

Serves 1. About 280 kcal/1175 kJ per serving.
Fat: 7 g • Carbohydrate: 41 g • Protein: 9 g

1 ripe nectarine
125 g/4½ oz low-fat yoghurt (1.5%)
1 tablespoon maple syrup
2 tablespoons oat flakes
1 teaspoon flaked (slivered) almonds

Wholemeal bread with herb quark

An ideal breakfast with plenty of fibre and protein which will satisfy your hunger while being very low in calories. This open sandwich also makes an ideal snack.

❶ Put the low-fat quark and milk in a bowl and stir until smooth. Season with sea salt, paprika and freshly ground pepper.

❷ Peel the onion and chop very finely. Wash the chives and chop finely. Wash the cress and dab dry. Chop half the cress finely and stir into the quark with the onion and herbs.

❸ Spread the herb quark on the slice of wholemeal bread and garnish with the rest of the cress.

Serves 1. About 260 kcal/1090 kJ per serving.
Fat: 3 g • Carbohydrate: 42 g • Protein: 16 g

70 g/3 oz low-fat quark

1 tablespoon milk

freshly ground pepper

1 pinch paprika

sea salt

1 small onion

½ bunch chives

2 tablespoons cress

2 slices wholemeal (wholewheat) bread

Pumpkin seed bread with orange marmalade

Lovers of bread and marmalade need not give it up in a low-fat diet, but the marmalade should have a high fruit content and contain as little sugar as possible. The sugar should be cane sugar, and such marmalade can be found in most health food shops.

❶ Spread the low-fat quark on the pumpkin seed bread and cover with the orange marmalade or other reduced-sugar fruit preserve.

❷ Peel the clementine or orange and cut into eight pieces. Arrange them with the bread on a plate.

Serves 1. About 160 kcal/670 kJ per serving.
Fat: 2 g • Carbohydrate: 28 g • Protein: 8 g

1 slice pumpkin seed bread

1 tablespoon low-fat quark

1 teaspoon marmalade or fruit spread as preferred

1 clementine or 1 small orange

Pear quark with crispbread

Quark is very versatile. It can be combined in all sorts of ways with fruit and cereals and has the advantage of containing very little fat. The yeast flakes can be bought in health food shops; they contain large amounts of B-vitamins which play a vital part in the formation of blood.

200 g/7 oz low-fat quark

2 tablespoons low-fat milk (1.5%)

1 pear

1 teaspoon honey

1 tablespoon spelt flakes

1 teaspoon yeast flakes

2 slices crispbread

❶ Put the low-fat quark and milk in a bowl and stir to make a smooth mixture. Wash the pear, cut into quarters and remove the core. Cut into very small cubes and stir into the quark.

❷ Sweeten the quark with honey and add the spelt flakes. Leave to stand for a few minutes.

❸ Put the pear yoghurt into a small bowl and sprinkle the yeast flakes on top. Serve with crispbread.

Serves 1. About 410 kcal/1720 kJ per serving.
Fat: 3 g • Carbohydrate: 54 g • Protein: 34 g

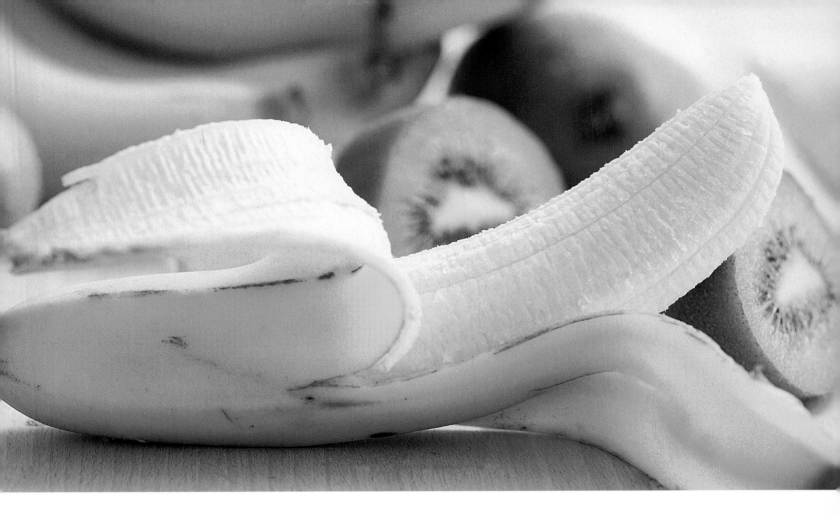

Yoghurt with fruit

The first meal of the day should always be varied and very light. Fresh fruit yoghurt is easy and quick to prepare and the fruit can be varied depending on the season and on what is available.

❶ Put the yoghurt, maple syrup and oat bran in a deep bowl and stir well. Wash the blackberries and dab dry. Peel the banana, cut into slices and sprinkle with lemon juice. Peel the kiwi fruit and cut it into slices .

❷ Garnish the yoghurt with the sliced banana and kiwi fruit. Fry the oat flakes without oil in a non-stick pan until light brown. Leave to cool and sprinkle over the fruit.

Serves 1. About 290 kcal/1220 kJ per serving.
Fat: 4 g • Carbohydrate: 46 g • Protein: 6 g

125 g/4½ oz low-fat yoghurt (1.5%)

1 teaspoon maple syrup

1 teaspoon oat bran

50 g/2 oz blackberries

½ banana

1 teaspoon lemon juice

1 kiwi fruit

2 tablespoons oat flakes

Scrambled egg with celery on bread

An ideal breakfast for the weekend when you have enough time to treat yourself to scrambled eggs. Because eggs are very high in cholesterol, one should not indulge in this kind of breakfast more than once or twice a week.

1 egg

salt

freshly ground pepper

½ bunch chives

1 teaspoon sunflower oil

1 slice wholemeal (wholewheat) spelt bread

1 teaspoon diet margarine

½ stick (stalk) celery with leaves

❶ Beat the egg in a bowl using a whisk and season with a little salt and pepper. Wash the chives, chop finely and add to the beaten egg.

❷ Heat the oil in a small non-stick pan, add the egg and allow to thicken for a few minutes over a low flame, stirring with a fork.

❸ Spread diet margarine on a slice of wholemeal (wholewheat) spelt bread. Remove the celery leaves, wash and put to one side. Wash the celery stick (stalk), cut into very thin slices and arrange on the bread. Serve on a plate with the scrambled egg and garnish with the celery leaves.

Serves 1. About 315 kcal/1320 kJ per serving.
Fat: 20 g • Carbohydrate: 26 g • Protein: 15 g

Bread with fresh strawberries

A delicious, light breakfast for everyone who loves strawberries: wholemeal (wholewheat) bread with fromage frais topped with a thick layer of sliced strawberries which can be seasoned with a little pepper.

2 slices wholemeal (whole grain) rye bread

2 teaspoons low-fat fromage frais

150 g/5 oz strawberries

1 teaspoon lemon juice

freshly ground black pepper

2 mint leaves

❶ Spread fromage frais on the slices of rye bread. Wash the strawberries, dab dry and remove the stalks. Cut the strawberries into slices and sprinkle with lemon juice.

❷ Arrange the sliced strawberries on the bread. Season with freshly ground pepper. Wash the mint leaves, dab dry, chop finely and sprinkle over the strawberries.

Serves 1. About 175 kcal/735 kJ per serving.
Fat: 6 g • Carbohydrate: 22 g • Protein: 5 g

Spicy hard-boiled (hard-cooked) egg spread

This spicy hard-boiled (hard-cooked) egg spread is ideal for Sunday brunch. It is particularly delicious served with wholemeal (wholewheat) spelt bread.

❶ Hard-boil (hard-cook) the egg, peel and cut into half. Leave to cool, then chop finely. Put the low-calorie salad cream, low-fat quark and lemon juice in a bowl and stir well. Carefully fold in the finely chopped hard-boiled egg.

❷ Drain the pickled gherkin and anchovy fillet, chop finely and add to salad cream and egg mixture. Season with chilli powder and pepper.

❸ Wash the chives, chop finely and add to the salad cream and egg mixture. Arrange on a plate and serve with a slice of wholemeal (wholewheat) bread.

Serves 1. About 295 kcal/1240 kJ per serving.
Fat: 12 g • Carbohydrate: 29 g • Protein: 18 g

1 egg
1 tablespoon low-fat salad cream
1 tablespoon low-fat quark
1 teaspoon lemon juice
1 small pickled gherkin
1 anchovy fillet (from the can)
1 pinch chilli powder
freshly ground pepper
½ bunch chives
1 wholemeal (wholewheat) roll

Snacks between meals

When you are suddenly ravenous, it is very tempting to grab a bar of chocolate or a sweet biscuit. But it's much better to enjoy one of the delicious snacks in this chapter, such as the light Coconut and carrot soup (page 75) or the delicate Wild rice and crab salad (page 65) instead. Both are quick and easy to prepare. In fact, you can combine two or three of these well-balanced, interesting low-fat snacks to make a main meal.

Vegetable fritters with mustard dip

This Asian "dip" is an absolute delight for "couch potatoes" who love to nibble. Fresh coriander is available in shops specialising in oriental food. However, it is also easy to grow coriander yourself in a pot on a window-sill.

1 small clove garlic

1 small bunch green coriander

1 tablespoon Dijon mustard

2 tablespoons sour cream

2 tablespoons low-fat yoghurt (1.5%)

1 teaspoon soy sauce

sea salt

freshly ground white pepper

150 g/5 oz potatoes

100 g/3½ oz celeriac

olive oil

❶ Peel the cloves of garlic and chop very finely. Wash the coriander carefully, shake dry and chop the leaves finely. Stir together the mustard, sour cream, yoghurt, soy sauce, cloves and chopped coriander. Season with salt and white pepper. Cover the dip and leave it in the refrigerator for two hours. Stir again and check the seasoning.

❷ Peel the potatoes and celeriac and cut into thin slices. This is best done with a vegetable slicer. Pour olive oil into a pan or deep-fryer and heat to 180°C (350°F). Add the sliced potatoes and celeriac and fry until golden-brown. Remove with a skimming ladle and drain dry on kitchen paper.

❸ Season the fritters with salt and serve immediately with the dip.

Serves 2. About 210 kcal/880 kJ per serving.
Fat: 14 g • Carbohydrate: 14 g • Protein: 4 g

Turkey kebab with peanut sauce

If prepared the day before, it will only take you 20 minutes to finish off this delicious dish, thus allowing you to enjoy more of your guests' company. Chicken breast can be used instead of turkey breast.

200 g/7 oz turkey breast

2 cloves garlic

1 piece fresh ginger (about 2 cm/¾ in long)

2 tablespoons soy sauce

1 pinch grated untreated lemon zest

1 pinch paprika

1 tablespoon acacia honey

1 pinch ground coriander

1 small onion

1 teaspoon groundnut oil

2 peppercorns

3 teaspoons peanut butter

sea salt

2 metal or wood skewers

❶ Rinse the turkey breast, wipe dry with kitchen paper and cut into bite-sized pieces. Peel the garlic and ginger. Chop the garlic finely and grate the ginger finely. Stir together the soy sauce, lemon zest, paprika, honey, coriander, garlic and ginger. Pour the marinade over the meat, cover and stand in the refrigerator for about four hours, or overnight.

❷ Peel the onion and cut into slices. Put the pieces of meat and onion slices on a kebab stick, alternating them. Heat the groundnut oil in a non-stick pan and fry the peppercorns briefly in it. Fry the kebabs on all sides in the hot oil for about 12 minutes. Remove from the saucepan and keep in a warm place.

❸ Mix the peanut butter with 100 ml/3½ fl oz (½ cup) water and the remaining marinade and stir well. Pour this mixture into the frying pan and stir with the cooking juices. Season the sauce with salt.

❹ Arrange the kebabs and peanut sauce on two plates and serve with basmati rice.

Serves 2. About 245 kcal/1030 kJ per serving.
Fat: 9 g • Carbohydrate: 10 g • Protein: 29 g

Tortillas stuffed with peppers and sweet corn

A Mexican snack which does not require much preparation. Tortillas can be bought ready-made in the supermarket and the vegetables are fried only very briefly.

1 small sweet pepper

1 small onion

1 teaspoon olive oil

100 g/3½ oz sweetcorn (from the can)

salt

cayenne pepper

some dried thyme

2 tortillas

❶ Clean the pepper, remove the stalk and seeds and cut into fine strips. Peel the onion and chop finely. Heat the olive oil in a non-stick pan and fry the pepper for about 5 minutes.

❷ Drain the sweet corn, add to the pan and heat up briefly. Season the vegetables with salt, cayenne pepper and thyme.

❸ Heat the tortillas in the oven for a few minutes following the instructions on the packet and remove from the oven. Place the vegetables on the hot tortillas and roll them up.

Serves 2. About 185 kcal/780 kJ per serving.
Fat: 9 g • Carbohydrate: 19 g • Protein: 4 g

Tomato salad with an open cheese sandwich

The tomatoes turn this small snack into a refreshing, fruity little meal. The open cheese sandwich can be made with any cheese of your choice – as long as it is low in fat – such as fat-reduced fromage frais or slices of low-fat hard cheese.

3 tomatoes

1 small clove garlic

½ leek

some sprigs of flat parsley

salt

freshly ground black pepper

1 tablespoon white wine vinegar

1–2 tablespoons vegetable stock (broth)

1 teaspoon olive oil

some sprigs of fresh thyme

1 slice ciabatta or other bread

20 g/¾ oz low-fat hard cheese or fromage frais

paprika

❶ Wash the tomatoes, remove the stalk, cut into slices and arrange on a flat platter. Peel the cloves of garlic and slice into thin slivers. Clean the leeks, wash and cut into thin slices.

❷ Wash the parsley, chop finely and sprinkle over the tomatoes. Prepare a dressing with a little salt, freshly ground pepper, vinegar, vegetable stock (broth) and olive oil and pour over the tomatoes. Wash the sprigs of thyme, dab them dry and garnish the tomatoes with them.

❸ Put a slice of cheese or spread some fromage frais on the bread and sprinkle with a little paprika.

Serves 1. About 260 kcal/1090 kJ per serving.
Fat: 9 g • Carbohydrate: 27 g • Protein: 5 g

Mixed sprout salad

You can make your own fresh sprouts from germinating grains but you can also buy them ready-made from the health food shop. These crisp sprouts contain a lot of vitamins while they germinate. The spiciest are radish and mustard sprouts.

1 bunch radishes

1 small courgette (zucchini)

½ bulb fennel

2 spring onions (scallions)

50 g/2 oz radish sprouts

50 g/2 oz alfalfa sprouts

1 tablespoon lemon juice

freshly ground pepper

1 tablespoon white wine vinegar

1 tablespoon vegetable stock (broth)

1 tablespoon thistle oil

1 small box cress

❶ Wash the radishes, top and tail and cut into slices. Wash, top and tail the courgettes and cut into sticks. Wash the fennel bulbs, top and tail and cut diagonally into fine strips. Wash the spring onions (scallions) and chop into slices. Put all these vegetables in a salad bowl.

❷ Wash the radish and alfalfa sprouts thoroughly and drain. Add to the vegetables in the salad bowl.

❸ Put the lemon juice, pepper, vinegar and stock (broth) in a small bowl and stir to make a smooth mixture. Whisk the thistle oil into this mixture and pour carefully over the vegetables and stir. Allow the salad to stand for 10 minutes. Cut the cress, wash it, dab it dry and sprinkle over the salad.

Serves 2. About 90 kcal/378KJ per serving.
Fat: 4 g • Carbohydrate: 7 g • Protein: 5 g

Indian rice salad

Oriental food is very filling but it contains very little fat. If you cook the rice and chicken breasts the day before and keep them in the refrigerator, this salad is very quick and easy to prepare. Brown rice contains much higher levels of vitamins and minerals than white rice and it takes longer to cook.

❶ Put the cooked brown rice in a bowl. Cut the chicken breast into strips, wash and prepare the spring onions (scallions), chop finely and add both to the rice.

❷ Peel the ginger, grate it finely and add to the lemon juice, vegetable stock (broth), soy sauce, curry and chilli powder. Stir to make a sauce which is then poured over the rice and chicken. Mix thoroughly and leave to stand for a few minutes.

❸ Fry the sesame seeds in a non-stick frying pan without any oil and sprinkle over the rice. Cut the apricot in half, remove the stone (pit), peel and cut into slices. Garnish the rice with the apricot slices and mint leaves.

Serves 2. About 290 kcal/1220KJ per serving.
Fat: 5 g • Carbohydrate: 36 g • Protein: 13 g

100 g/3½ oz cooked rice
  (about 30–40 g/1–1½ oz
  uncooked weight)

50 g/2 oz cooked chicken breast

2 spring onions (scallions)

1 small piece root ginger

1 tablespoon lemon juice

1 tablespoon vegetable stock
  (broth)

1 tablespoon soy sauce

½ teaspoon curry powder

1 pinch chilli powder

1 teaspoon sesame seeds

1 apricot

some leaves of mint

Ham open sandwich with rocket

A small, nutritious meal, ideal for midday. The rocket salad with its slightly peppery taste is delicious and the wholemeal (wholewheat) bread contains very little fat but a lot of fibre.

1 bunch rocket (about 80 g/3 oz)

1 small carrot

½ red sweet pepper

1 tablespoon lemon juice

freshly ground pepper

1 tablespoon balsamic vinegar

1 teaspoon olive oil

½ bunch chives

1 slice wholemeal rye bread

1 teaspoon diet margarine

2 thin slices Parma ham

❶ Wash and prepare the salad and the vegetables. Cut the carrots and pepper into matchsticks and put in a small salad bowl together with the rocket.

❷ Make a salad dressing with lemon juice, pepper, balsamic vinegar and olive oil. Wash the chives, chop and add to the dressing.

❸ Spread some diet margarine on a slice of wholemeal rye bread and put a slice of Parma ham on top. Pour the dressing over the salad just before serving and mix carefully.

Serves 2. About 270 kcal/1130 kJ per serving.
Fat: 16 g • Carbohydrate: 24 g • Protein: 10 g

Beetroot (red beet) salad

You can buy ready-cooked beetroot (red beet) in the shops – steamed and vacuum-packed, it has preserved all its important minerals and vitamins such as vitamin C. Combined with oranges and chicory, it makes a delicious salad which is also very filling.

100 g/3½ oz steamed beetroot (red beet)

1 bulb chicory

1 orange

salt

freshly ground pepper

1 teaspoon balsamic vinegar

½ carton low-fat yoghurt (1.5%)

1 teaspoon chopped walnuts

1 slice wholemeal (wholewheat) bread

❶ Cut the beetroot (red beet) in half and cut into slices. Divide the leaves of the chicory and arrange them decoratively in a soup plate.

❷ Peel the orange and divide into segments. Arrange the beetroot (red beet) slices on the chicory leaves. Mix salt, pepper, balsamic vinegar and yoghurt together to make a dressing.

❸ Pour the dressing over the vegetables, sprinkle chopped walnuts on top and serve with a slice of wholemeal bread.

Serves 2. About 285 kcal/1180 kJ per serving.
Fat: 3 g • Carbohydrate: 45 g • Protein: 9 g

Gratiné goat's cheese on a bed of melon

A refreshing, summery snack with a sweet and sour dressing. Served with some crisp white bread, this refined salad is also ideal for a light evening meal.

1 Wash and prepare the mangetout (snow peas). Cut the pods in half. Peel the carrots and cut them into thin slices. Heat up the chicken stock (broth) and cook the vegetables in it for about 5 minutes. Drain them and reserve the cooking liquid.

2 Preheat the oven to 200°C (400°F), Gas mark 6. Remove the seeds from the melon, cut into slices and peel. Put the cheeses in a small ovenproof dish, sprinkle with thyme and pour 1 teaspoon maple syrup on top. Bake the cheeses in the oven for about 10 minutes until they begin to melt.

3 Mix the mustard, remaining maple syrup, cider vinegar, 1 tablespoon stock (broth), herb salt, pepper and capers together to make a dressing and whisk in the walnut oil.

4 Arrange the salad and melon slices on two plates and put the cheeses on top. Pour the dressing over the salad. Sprinkle chopped walnuts on top or cut Parma ham into strips and garnish the salad with them.

Serves 2. About 295 kcal/1240 kJ per serving.
Fat: 15 g • Carbohydrate: 25 g • Protein: 6 g

80 g/3 oz mangetout (snow peas)

2 young carrots

50 ml/1½ fl oz (3 tablespoons) chicken stock (broth)

½ ripe honeydew melon

2 small goat's cheeses (each 50 g/2 oz)

½ teaspoon fresh thyme leaves

2 teaspoons maple syrup

1 teaspoon medium strong mustard

1 tablespoon cider vinegar

herb salt

freshly ground pepper

1 teaspoon capers

1 teaspoon walnut oil

2 tablespoons chopped walnuts or 1 slice Parma ham

2 tomatoes

2 red sweet peppers

1 chilli pepper

1 clove garlic

1 onion

1 tablespoon olive oil

60 g/2 oz (¼ cup) brown rice

1 litre/13/4 pints (4½ cups)
    vegetable stock (broth)

salt

freshly ground pepper

some fresh oregano

1 bunch chives

Paprika and rice soup

Soups should be part of your weekly meal plan – they provide a lot of liquid and very little fat, as well as being quick and easy to prepare. If you add brown rice to the vegetables, this soup becomes a complete meal in itself.

❶ Make a cross-shaped incision in the tomatoes, remove the stalk, blanch briefly in boiling water and peel. Cut the tomatoes into eight pieces. Wash and prepare the peppers and cut into thin strips. Cut the chilli lengthways, remove the seeds and cut into small pieces.

❷ Peel the garlic and onion and chop finely. Heat the olive oil in a large saucepan and fry the garlic and onion until transparent. Add the vegetables and fry briefly with the onion and garlic.

❸ Wash the brown rice and add to the vegetables. Pour in the stock (broth), cover and simmer for about 20–25 minutes over a low heat until the rice is cooked.

❹ Season the soup with salt and pepper. Wash the oregano and chives , chop finely and sprinkle over the soup.

Serves 2. About 215 kcal/900 kJ per serving.

Fat: 8 g • Carbohydrate: 30 g • Protein: 5 g

Brussels sprouts and leek soup

Brussels sprouts are a delicious winter vegetable which can be used to make delicious, nutritious soups and soufflés. Served with a slice of wholemeal (wholewheat) bread, this light soup makes a healthy snack or a light meal.

❶ Wash and prepare the Brussels sprouts and cut them into half. Wash and prepare the leeks and celery and cut them into fine strips. Peel the onions and chop finely.

❷ Heat the olive oil in a large saucepan and fry the onion until transparent. Add the vegetables and fry them briefly. Pour in the stock (broth), cover and simmer the vegetables for about 20 minutes over a low heat.

❸ Season the soup with salt, grated nutmeg and freshly ground pepper. Wash the basil, cut the leaves into fine strips and sprinkle over the soup. Pour the soup in two bowls and sprinkle with Parmesan.

Serves 2. About 118 kcal/495 kJ per serving.
Fat: 4 g • Carbohydrate: 10 g • Protein: 9 g

250 g/9 oz Brussels sprouts

2 leeks

1 stick (stalk) celery

1 onion

1 teaspoon olive oil

400 ml/14 fl oz (1¾ cups) vegetable stock (broth)

sea salt

freshly grated nutmeg

freshly ground pepper

1 bunch basil

1 tablespoon grated Parmesan

Coconut and carrot soup

This exquisite soup is a real visual delight and will provide you with large amounts of carotene which converts into the vitally important vitamin A. Because the body can only absorb this vitamin in combination with fat, you should always add a little oil or cream – just a teaspoon is sufficient!

❶ Wash and prepare the spring onions (scallions) and chop them finely. Heat the sunflower oil in a saucepan and fry the spring onions (scallions) lightly. Wash and prepare the carrots, peel and cut into slices. Add the carrots to the onions and fry for a few minutes, stirring constantly.

❷ Sprinkle lemon juice over the carrots, add the vegetable stock (broth) and simmer for about 15 minutes. Purée the vegetables in a blender, add the coconut milk and heat the soup again briefly. If the soup is too thick, add a little more vegetable stock (broth).

❸ Season the soup with curry powder, salt and cayenne pepper. Wash the coriander, chop the leaves coarsely and sprinkle over the soup.

Serves 1. About 118 kcal/495 kJ per serving.
Fat: 6 g • Carbohydrate: 11 g • Protein: 2 g

1 spring onion (scallion)

1 teaspoon sunflower oil

3 large carrots

1 teaspoon lemon juice

125 ml/4 fl oz (½ cup) vegetable stock (broth)

50 ml/1½ fl oz (3 tablespoons) coconut milk

1 pinch curry powder

salt

cayenne pepper

some fresh coriander leaves

Spicy creamed pumpkin and mustard soup

A real "Halloween" soup, lightly seasoned with mustard and puréed to give it a creamy texture. Hokkaido pumpkins are the best for this purpose because their flesh is very tasty and deep orange in colour. However, this soup can also be prepared with other kinds of pumpkins such as the large garden pumpkin.

1 piece pumpkin (about 200 g/7 oz)

1 potato (50 g/2 oz)

1 onion

1 clove garlic

1 teaspoon sunflower oil

250 ml/8 fl oz (1 cup) vegetable stock (broth)

75 ml/3 fl oz (⅜ cup) cream

1 tablespoon crème fraîche

3 teaspoons medium mustard

sea salt

freshly ground white pepper

2 teaspoons pumpkin seed oil

❶ Peel the pumpkin, remove the seeds and cut the flesh into dice. Peel the potatoes and cut into cubes. Peel the onion and garlic and chop finely.

❷ Heat the oil in a saucepan and fry the onion until transparent. Add the garlic and fry briefly with the onion. Add the diced pumpkin and potato and continue frying. Pour in the stock (broth), cover and simmer the vegetables for about 15 minutes.

❸ Take two tablespoons of diced pumpkin and put to one side. Add the cream and crème fraîche to the soup and purée with a hand-mixer. Season with mustard, salt and white pepper.

❹ Pour the soup into two bowls, garnish with the diced pumpkin and sprinkle pumpkin seed oil over it.

Serves 2. About 260 kcal/1090 kJ per serving.
Fat: 17 g • Carbohydrate: 11 g • Protein: 2 g

Stuffed sesame pancakes (crepes)

These are exquisite pancakes (crepes) which also satisfy all modern health requirements, containing many vitamins and minerals as well as fibre. The vegetables used for the filling can be varied according to the season. If you are in a hurry, you can also use deep-frozen vegetables.

❶ Make a pancake (crepe) batter with the egg, flour, mineral water, a pinch of salt and sesame seeds. Cover and leave to stand for 10 minutes.

❷ Drain the corn on the cob. Wash and prepare the pepper, sugar peas and cauliflower and cut into small pieces. Heat 1 teaspoon olive oil in a saucepan, add the vegetables and fry them. Pour in the stock (broth) and season with salt and pepper. Cover and simmer for about 10 minutes over a low heat.

❸ For each pancake (crepe), heat one teaspoon olive oil in a non-stick frying pan and make the two pancakes (crepes), one after the other. Put the cooked vegetables on the pancakes (crepes), roll them up and arrange them on two warmed plates. Serve with the chilli sauce.

Serves 2. About 290 kcal/1220 kJ per serving.

Fat: 15 g • Carbohydrate: 23 g • Protein: 7 g

1 egg

1 tablespoon spelt flour

4 tablespoons low-fat milk (1.5%)

3 tablespoons sparkling mineral water

sea salt

1 teaspoon sesame seeds

50 g/2 oz small corn on the cob

½ red sweet pepper

50 g/2 oz sugar peas

100 g/3½ oz cauliflower florets

3 teaspoons olive oil

freshly ground pepper

1 tablespoon vegetable stock (broth)

sweet-and-sour chilli sauce

Fish and meat dishes

Carefully prepared lean meat and low-fat fish are important sources of valuable unsaturated fatty acids. To give just two examples, Zander with braised carrots and mushrooms (page 86) and Pork fillet (tenderloin) with peach chutney (page 102) are not only delicious but also very healthy and low in calories.

Fish on a bed of rice and Swiss chard

A quick and easy dish. The fish is sprinkled with lemon juice and cooked on a bed of rice and Swiss chard.

❶ Peel the garlic and chop finely. Heat the olive oil in a large non-stick pan and fry the garlic in it.

❷ Wash the rice and add to the pan. Fry for a few minutes, stirring all the time. Pour the vegetable stock (broth) into the pan with the garlic and rice. Season with salt and pepper.

❸ Wash and prepare the Swiss chard and cut into strips 2 cm/¾ in wide. Add the Swiss chard to the rice in the pan. Cover and cook for about 10 minutes. Add more vegetable stock (broth) if necessary.

❹ After about 10 minutes, put the fish fillets on top of the rice and Swiss chard mixture. Sprinkle with lemon juice. Cover and cook for a further 5–10 minutes until the fish is cooked.

❺ Wash the parsley, pat dry and chop the leaves finely. Arrange the rice and Swiss chard on two plates with the fish and sprinkle with the chopped parsley.

Serves 2. About 410 kcal/1720 kJ per serving.
Fat: 7 g • Carbohydrate: 47 g • Protein: 20 g

1 clove garlic

1 tablespoon olive oil

120 g/4 oz easy-cook rice

250 ml/8 fl oz (1 cup) vegetable
 stock (broth)

salt

freshly ground pepper

250 g/9 oz Swiss chard

300 g/10 oz cod or pollack fillets

juice of 1 lemon

½ bunch parsley

Stuffed chicken breasts

These crisp roast chicken fillets are filled with an exotic stuffing made of peppers, coconut and the zest of a lime. Delicious served with rice, especially brown rice which is full of vitamins and fibre!

1 small red sweet pepper

1 small yellow sweet pepper

2 shallots

1 clove garlic

1 tablespoon olive oil

2 tablespoons grated coconut

zest and juice of 1 untreated lime

sea salt

freshly ground pepper

2 chicken breast fillets (each 200 g/7 oz)

1 teaspoon Tabasco sauce

½ teaspoon paprika

1 teaspoon marmalade

parsley

❶ Pre-heat the oven to 180°C (350°F), Gas mark 4. Wash and prepare the peppers and cut into small cubes. Peel the shallots and garlic and chop finely. Heat the oil in a non-stick pan and fry the shallots until transparent. Add the garlic and fry briefly. Stir in the diced peppers and cook for 5 minutes more. Stir in 1½ tablespoons grated coconut and the zest of a lime. Season with salt and pepper.

❷ Wash the chicken breasts, wipe dry with kitchen paper and make an incision in one side to make a pocket in both chicken breasts. Fill with the pepper mixture and close the openings with two cocktail sticks . Put them in a shallow ovenproof dish. Add ½ teaspoon paprika and 1 teaspoon water to the Tabasco sauce and stir to make the marinade. Cover the chicken with marinade.

❸ Roast the chicken breasts in the oven for about 25 minutes. Remove from the dish and keep in a warm place. Deglaze the cooking juices with lime juice and orange marmalade. Season with salt and pepper.

❹ Arrange the stuffed chicken breasts on two warmed plates and pour the sauce over them. Garnish with the rest of the grated coconut and parsley.

Serves 2. About 365 kcal/1530 kJ per serving.
Fat: 14 g • Carbohydrate: 6 g • Protein: 50 g

Lamb fillets with bulgur and okra

Okra is also known as lady's fingers. It contains a jelly-like mass which remains intact when pre-cooked in lightly salted water mixed with vinegar, and then processed according to the recipe.

❶ Rinse the lamb fillet and wipe dry. Wash the okra and cut off the dry ends. Pre-cook lightly in a mixture of water and vinegar. Drain well. Chop the okra finely. Peel the carrots, wash the celery sticks and cut both into thin slices.

❷ Heat the oil in a deep pan or wok and brown the lamb fillet over a high heat. Season with salt and pepper. Remove from the pan and keep warm.

❸ Add the vegetables, bay leaf and cloves to the pan, cover and braise for about 10 minutes. Dice the apricots, add to the vegetables and braise for a further 5 minutes.

❹ Rinse the bulgur in a colander. Bring the vegetable stock (broth) to the boil and add the bulgur. Bring to the boil again and simmer for about another 25 minutes over a very low heat until almost all the liquid has evaporated.

❺ Cut the lamb fillets into slices, add to the vegetables and warm up again. Season with salt, pepper and vinegar. Arrange the lamb fillets with the vegetables and bulgur on two warmed plates. Garnish with the lemon balm leaves.

Serves 2. About 510 kcal/2140 kJ per serving.
Fat: 11 g • Carbohydrate: 59 g • Protein: 38 g

250 g/9 oz lamb fillet

120 g/4 oz okra

3 carrots

3 sticks (stalks) celery

1 tablespoon olive oil

herb salt

freshly ground pepper

1 bay leaf

3 cloves

5 dried apricots

150 g/5 oz bulgur

350 ml/12 fl oz (1½ cups) vegetable stock (broth)

1–2 tablespoons white wine vinegar

some leaves of lemon balm

Ginger chicken
with curried rice

White poultry meat is very low in calories and can be prepared in many ways. Here chicken breasts are the basis of a delicately spicy dish, enhanced with the addition of oriental herbs and spices.

120 g/4 oz (generous ½ cup) easy-cook rice

salt

1 tablespoon curry powder

2 spring onions (scallions)

1 small piece fresh ginger root

1 red sweet pepper

1 teaspoon sunflower oil

2 chicken breast fillets

1 teaspoon lemon juice

1 teaspoon chilli powder

125 ml/4 fl oz (½ cup) vegetable stock (broth)

3 teaspoons coconut milk

100 g/3½ oz bamboo shoots (from a jar or can)

1 bunch fresh coriander

❶ Bring 250 ml/8 fl oz (1 cup) water to the boil in a saucepan. Add the salt, the curry powder and the rice and cook for about 15–20 minutes until ready, adding some more hot water while cooking if necessary. At the end of the cooking time all the liquid should have been absorbed by the rice.

❷ Clean the spring onions (scallions) and chop into small pieces. Peel the ginger and grate finely. Clean and wash the red pepper and cut into strips.

❸ Heat the oil in a large pan, add the spring onions (scallions) and braise lightly. Sprinkle lemon juice over the chicken breasts, add them to the spring onions (scallions) in the pan and fry vigorously on each side for about 1 minute. Add the grated ginger, the pepper cut into strips and the chilli powder; cook briefly. Add the vegetable stock (broth) and coconut milk. Cover and cook for a further 5–10 minutes until ready.

❹ Add the bamboo shoots just before the end of cooking. Wash the coriander, dab dry and chop the leaves finely. Arrange the chicken on two plates with its sauce and curried rice. Sprinkle with coriander.

Serves 2. About 435 kcal/1830 kJ per serving.
Fat: 7 g • Carbohydrate: 50 g • Protein: 37 g

Tuna and celeriac with pasta

Pasta and vegetables – the ideal combination for low-fat cuisine! The dish is enriched by the addition of tuna.

200 g/7 oz wholemeal (wholewheat) pasta

salt

1 onion

1 teaspoon sunflower oil

1 small piece celeriac

some grated nutmeg

125 ml/4 fl oz (½ cup) low-fat milk (1.5%)

125 g/4½ oz tuna fish without oil (from the can)

freshly ground white pepper

1 bunch chives

❶ Heat about 500 ml/17 fl oz (2¼ cups) water in a large saucepan. Season with salt, add the pasta and cook following the instructions on the packet.

❷ Peel the onion and chop finely. Heat the oil in a casserole and fry the onion until transparent. Peel the celeriac and cut into small cubes. Add to the casserole and season with a little grated nutmeg. Add the low-fat milk, cover and the cook the vegetables for about 10 minutes.

❸ Drain the tuna, shred with a fork and add to the celeriac. Heat briefly. Season with salt and freshly ground pepper.

❹ Wash the chives and chop finely. Drain the pasta and arrange on two plates, garnish with the vegetables and sprinkle the chives on top.

Serves 2. About 560 kcal/2350 kJ per serving.
Fat: 18 g • Carbohydrate: 69 g • Protein: 33 g

Turkey schnitzel with kohlrabi and asparagus

Lean poultry, lamb or beef are also part of low-fat cuisine and play an important role in many recipes. But proper preparation is vital. Very little fat must be used and the meat should be cooked or fried in a non-stick pan. Larger pieces should be braised slowly for a long time.

❶ Put the lemon juice, herbs of Provence and olive oil in a bowl and stir to make a marinade. Coat the meat with this and leave to stand for 1 hour.

❷ Wash and prepare the kohlrabi and asparagus. Cut the kohlrabi into cubes and the asparagus into pieces 3 cm/1¼ in long. Put the vegetables in a casserole and pour the vegetable stock (broth) over them. Cover and braise for 5–10 minutes until tender.

❸ Heat a non-stick pan, add the turkey schnitzel and the marinade and cook for about 3–5 minutes on each side.

❹ Add crème fraîche to the vegetables and season with salt and pepper. Remove the schnitzel from the pan, add a little more pepper and arrange on a large platter with the vegetables.

Serves 2. About 290 kcal/1220 kJ per serving.
Fat: 10 g • Carbohydrate: 7 g • Protein: 40 g

**1 small turkey schnitzel
  (about 150 g/5 oz)**

1 tablespoon lemon juice

1 teaspoon herbs of Provence

1 teaspoon olive oil

1 small kohlrabi

150 g/5 oz green asparagus

**3 tablespoons vegetable stock
  (broth)**

1 teaspoon crème fraîche

freshly ground white pepper

salt

Zander fillet with rice, plums and fennel

Zander, one of the finest freshwater fish, has a delicate, juicy white flesh. It tastes best in the autumn and winter when prepared freshly caught. Served with basmati rice and sweet and sour autumn vegetables, it is a sophisticated dish which will delight any guest.

100 g/3½ oz basmati rice

sea salt

1 bulb fennel

2 shallots

1 piece fresh ginger (about
   3 cm/1¼ in long)

120 g/4 oz plums

400 g/14 oz zander fillets

juice of 1 lime

2 teaspoons cooking oil

freshly ground pepper

1 teaspoon acacia honey

soy sauce

❶ Cook the rice in salted water following the instructions on the packet. Wash and prepare the fennel, then cut into thin strips. Peel the shallots and ginger and chop finely. Rub the plums clean with kitchen paper, remove the stones and cut into small pieces.

❷ Rinse the zander fillet, wipe dry, cut into bite-sized pieces and sprinkle with the juice of ½ a lime.

❸ Heat the oil in a pan and fry the zander fillet on both sides in the hot oil. Season with salt and pepper. Add the fennel, shallots, ginger and plums and cook for about 6 minutes. Season with the rest of the lime juice, salt, pepper, honey and soy sauce.

❹ Arrange the zander fillet with the plums and fennel on two warmed dishes and serve with basmati rice.

Serves 2. About 465 kcal/1950 kJ per serving.
Fat: 8 g • Carbohydrate: 54 g • Protein: 45 g

Chicken in a crisp chilli coating with peach and parsley sauce

Chilli lovers will use 2 teaspoons of chilli powder to make the chilli paste. These hot, spicy chicken breasts are delicious served with bulgur, an oriental side-dish made from pre-cooked cracked wheat grains.

1 Pre-heat the oven to 200°C (400°F), Gas mark 6.

2 Put the vinegar, chilli powder, paprika powder, thyme, cumin, pepper and salt in a cup and stir to make a marinade. Wash the chicken fillets, wipe them dry with kitchen paper and coat the chicken breasts with the marinade.

3 Cover a baking sheet with greaseproof paper, put the chicken breasts on it and bake for about 35 minutes in the oven until brown and crispy.

4 Meanwhile prepare the sauce. Blanch the peach, peel, cut in half, remove the stone (pit) and cut the flesh into small cubes. Peel the shallots and chop finely. Stir in the diced peach, chopped shallot, parsley and lime juice. Serve with the crispy chicken breasts.

Serves 2. About 160 kcal/360 kJ per serving.

Fat: 1 g • Carbohydrate: 12 g • Protein: 7 g

1 tablespoon sherry vinegar
1 teaspoon chilli powder
1 teaspoon paprika
1 teaspoon dried thyme
½ teaspoon ground cumin
1 pinch freshly ground pepper
herb salt
2 chicken breast fillets
1 ripe peach
1 shallot
1 tablespoon chopped parsley
2 tablespoons lime juice

Provençal lamb
with olives

This is a delicious recipe for a light Sunday roast, braised in an aromatic sauce made with fragrant herbs and tomatoes. Do not overdo the olives because they contain a lot of oil.

❶ Put the lemon juice, pepper, herbs and olive oil in a bowl and stir to make a smooth marinade. Coat the loin of lamb with the marinade and leave to stand for 2–3 hours.

❷ Heat a large, non-stick casserole and briefly sear the marinated loin of lamb all over.

❸ Peel and finely chop the onion and garlic. Wash the tomatoes, remove the stalk and cut into quarters. Add the tomatoes, onion and garlic to the casserole, cover and braise for about 45 minutes over a low heat.

❹ Wash the potatoes and brush them clean. Bring 1 litre/1¾ pints (4½ cups) water to the boil in a large saucepan, season with a little salt and cook the potatoes for about 8–10 minutes over a low flame until done. Check with a fork to see that the potatoes are cooked enough and drain immediately.

❺ Next add the olives to the casserole and season with salt and pepper. Wash the thyme, dab dry and chop the leaves finely.

❻ Peel the potatoes and arrange with the meat and vegetables on a dish. Garnish with the thyme.

Serves 2. About 265 kcal/1110 kJ per serving.
Fat: 12 g • Carbohydrate: 6 g • Protein: 34 g

1 tablespoon lemon juice

freshly ground pepper

2 teaspoons dried herbs of Provence

1 teaspoon olive oil

300 g/10 oz loin of lamb

1 large onion

1 clove garlic

300 g/10 oz tomatoes

300 g/10 oz potatoes

salt

2 tablespoons black olives

fresh thyme

Chicken on a bed of vegetables and wild rice

Wild rice with its exquisitely nutty taste is served here with fresh vegetables and chicken to make a light meal, full of vitamins. It is particularly quick if you buy ready-roasted chicken breasts and cook the rice the day before, keeping it overnight in the refrigerator.

100 g/3½ oz mixed wild rice

sea salt

200 g/7 oz chicken breast fillets

4 teaspoon olive oil

freshly ground pepper

75 g/3 oz button mushrooms

75 g/3 oz oyster mushrooms

1 small cucumber

½ red sweet pepper

½ yellow sweet pepper

2 teaspoons sherry vinegar

1 tablespoon chopped parsley

1 teaspoon capers

❶ Cook the wild rice in salted water following the instructions on the packet and leave to cool. Meanwhile, wash the chicken breasts, wipe dry and cook for about 12 minutes in 1 teaspoon hot oil, turning the chicken over regularly. Season with salt and pepper. Remove from the pan.

❷ Clean the mushrooms, rub clean with kitchen paper and cut in slices or strips. Fry briefly in the cooking fat and put to one side.

❸ Peel the cucumber and cut into thin slices. Wash and prepare the peppers and cut into thin strips. Mix the remaining olive oil, vinegar, parsley and capers and season with salt and pepper.

❹ Mix the wild rice, mushrooms, vegetables and vinaigrette and arrange on two plates. Cut the chicken breasts into slices and place on top of the rice and vegetables.

Serves 2. About 410 kcal/1720 kJ per serving.
Fat: 13 g • Carbohydrate: 46 g • Protein: 32 g

Rabbit fillet with Chinese noodles and mushrooms

Rabbit has a similar taste to chicken and is very easy to digest. Wild rabbit is particularly tasty. This autumn dish is quick and easy to prepare. The recipe can be varied by using other kinds of mushrooms, such as Shiitake mushrooms.

❶ Put the noodles in a bowl and pour boiling salted water over them. Leave to stand briefly and drain. Heat the oil in a wok or deep pan and fry the rabbit for 6–8 minutes, turning the meat regularly. Season with salt and pepper, remove from the pan and keep warm.

❷ Wash and prepare the spring onions (scallions) and cut into rings. Peel the pears, remove the core and dice small. Cut the chilli lengthways, remove the seeds and cut into fine strips. Clean the mushrooms and cut into small pieces. Add the pears, spring onions (scallions), chilli and mushrooms to the cooking fat. Strip the thyme leaves from the stems and add to the pan. Cook this mixture for 8–10 minutes.

❸ Cut the rabbit fillets into slices. Add them to the vegetables together with the noodles. Stir well and heat the mixture again. Season with salt and pepper and serve on two warmed plates.

Serves 2. About 420 kcal/1765 kJ per serving.
Fat: 11 g • Carbohydrate: 50 g • Protein: 28 g

200 g/7 oz Chinese noodles
sea salt
1 tablespoon sunflower oil
250 g/9 oz rabbit fillets
freshly ground pepper
4 spring onions (scallions)
1 ripe pear
1 mild red chilli pepper
100 g/3½ oz mixed mushrooms
2 sprigs thyme

Broccoli and potatoes with chicken breasts

Cream-based sauces are taboo in low-fat cuisine, but there is a trick which allows you to make creamy sauces. Broccoli and potatoes are cooked with milk instead of cream so that the calorie count is hardly affected.

5 potatoes

5 small carrots

300 g/10 oz broccoli

1 onion

125 ml/4 fl oz (½ cup) vegetable stock (broth)

200 ml/7 fl oz (⅞ cup) low-fat milk (1.5%)

grated nutmeg

salt

freshly ground pepper

1 tablespoon sunflower oil

250 g/9 oz chicken breast fillets

some fresh chervil leaves

❶ Peel the carrots and potatoes and cut into sticks. Wash and prepare the broccoli and divide into florets. Peel the onions and chop finely.

❷ Bring the vegetable stock (broth) to the boil in a medium-sized saucepan, add the vegetables, cover and cook for about 10 minutes. Add the milk and grated nutmeg and reduce the milk-based sauce for about 5 minutes to thicken it. Season the vegetables with salt and freshly ground pepper.

❸ Heat the sunflower oil in a non-stick pan. Cut the chicken breasts in strips and fry on all sides until golden brown. Season with salt and pepper.

❹ Wash the chervil, dab dry and chop the leaves finely. Arrange the vegetables and chicken on two plates, pour the sauce on top and sprinkle with chervil.

Serves 2. About 465 kcal/1950 kJ per serving.

Fat: 7 g • Carbohydrate: 42 g • Protein: 42 g

Pork fillet (tenderloin) with peach chutney

Chutney originates from India; it is a very spicy, sweet-and-sour sauce which can be made from a variety of fruit. It is usually served with meat. If in a rush, use ready-made chutney.

250 g/9 oz pork fillet (tenderloin)

salt

freshly ground pepper

1 teaspoon cooking oil

2 peaches

2 tablespoons peach preserve

1 teaspoon white wine vinegar

1 teaspoon soy sauce

1 mild red chilli pepper

❶ Wash the pork fillet (tenderloin) and wipe dry. Cut it into slices 2.5 cm/1 in thick and flatten with the palm of your hand. Season the fillets on both sides with salt and pepper. Heat the oil in a non-stick pan and fry the pieces briskly on both sides for 3 minutes each side. Remove from the pan and keep in a warm place.

❷ For the chutney: Blanch the peaches, peel, remove the stones (pits) and dice. Put the peaches, vinegar, soy sauce and peach preserve in a saucepan and stir well. Simmer over medium heat for 5–7 minutes. The chutney should have a thick consistency.

❸ Arrange the slices of pork fillet on two warmed plates and garnish with the chutney. Serve with rice.

Serves 2. About 265 kcal/1110 kJ per serving.
Fat: 6 g • Carbohydrate: 23 g • Protein: 28 g

Chicken breasts with vegetables and Hollandaise sauce

This dish of tasty winter vegetables combined with tender chicken breastz is enhanced by the addition of smoked salmon and salmon roe, all in a creamy butter sauce. It is ideally suited for a special occasion.

❶ Wash the chicken fillets, wipe them dry and season with herb salt and pepper. Heat the butter in a small pan and fry the chicken breasts for 6 minutes on each side until golden brown.

❷ Peel and dice the carrots. Clean, wash and prepare the leeks and cut into rings. Peel and dice the potatoes. Cook the vegetables in a little salted water for about 15 minutes until tender.

❸ Cut half the smoked salmon into small dice and make small rosettes from the remaining salmon. Warm the Hollandaise sauce over a low heat, stirring continuously.

❹ Arrange the finely diced salmon in the middle of two plates. Put the chicken breasts with the Hollandaise sauce on top with the vegetables next to them. Garnish with the salmon rosettes, parsley and salmon roe. Serve immediately.

Serves 2. About 540 kcal/2270 kJ per serving.

Fat: 30 g • Carbohydrate: 20 g • Protein: 42 g

2 halved chicken breast fillets

herb salt

freshly ground pepper

1 tablespoon butter

2 carrots

1 leek

150 g/5 oz waxy potatoes

80 g/3 oz smoked fish

200 ml/7 fl oz (⅞ cup) Hollandaise sauce

curly-leaved parsley

1 teaspoon salmon roe

Beef with mushrooms

Oriental meat dishes are usually low in fat because they usually consist of a combination of vegetables, mushrooms and meat cooked in a non-stick pan or wok without any oil.

250 g/9 oz fillet of beef

3 tablespoons Marsala

3 tablespoons soy sauce

1 teaspoon cornflour
   (corn starch)

1 small piece fresh root ginger

1 clove garlic

2 small onions

100 g/3½ oz mushrooms

salt

pepper

1 teaspoon sesame seeds

❶ Cut the beef fillet into thin strips. Put the Marsala, soy sauce and cornflour (corn starch) in a small bowl, stir and pour over the meat. Leave to stand for 30 minutes.

❷ Peel the ginger and chop finely. Peel the garlic and onions and cut into thin slices. Prepare the mushrooms and wipe clean with kitchen paper to remove all grit. Cut into quarters.

❸ Heat a non-stick pan without any oil, remove the meat from the marinade and fry briskly over a high heat for about 3 minutes, stirring continuously. Season with salt and pepper. Put the marinade to one side.

❹ Add the ginger, garlic, onions and mushrooms and fry briefly with the meat over a high heat. Next add the marinade and simmer for 3 minutes more. Season with salt and pepper.

❺ Fry the sesame seeds in a small pan without any oil until light brown. Arrange the meat with the sauce on two plates. Sprinkle with sesame seeds and serve with rice.

Serves 2. About 255 kcal/1070 kJ per serving.
Fat: 9 g • Carbohydrate: 10 g • Protein: 34 g

Pasta, rice and vegetable dishes

Not only vegetarians will be tempted by these delicious Vegetable kebabs with a spicy dip (page 128). Low-fat cuisine will also appeal to meat lovers, offering them many tasty alternatives which contain very little fat. Try for instance the nourishing Spelt grain risotto (page 115) or the Kohlrabi gratin with wild garlic sauce (page 130). Delicious!

Potato soup

A nourishing dish which will satisfy the largest appetite without piling on the calories, because this nourishing potato soup is made with low-fat fish. An important tip in low-fat cooking: vegetable stews can be made creamy if you add milk to the vegetable stock (broth).

3 large floury potatoes

2 carrots

1 parsley root

2 sticks (stalks) celery

750 ml/1¼ pints (3½ cups) vegetable stock (broth)

250 ml/8 fl oz (1 cup) low-fat milk (1.5%)

freshly ground pepper

salt

some dried marjoram

200 g/7 oz low-fat sea fish (for instance rosefish)

some sprigs of parsley

❶ Peel the potatoes, carrots and parsley root. Cut the potatoes into thin slices. Cut the carrots and parsley root into large cubes. Wash the celery and chop coarsely.

❷ Heat the vegetable stock (broth) and milk in a large saucepan and add the vegetables. Cook for about 10–15 minutes until ready.

❸ Purée the vegetable soup with a hand-mixer and season with salt, pepper and marjoram.

❹ Cut the fish into thin strips and add to the soup. Cook over a low heat for about 5 minutes. Wash the parsley, dab dry, chop the leaves and sprinkle over the soup.

Serves 2. About 270 kcal/1130 kJ per serving.

Fat: 5 g • Carbohydrate: 28 g • Protein: 25 g

Spelt grain risotto

These spelt grains have a particularly nutty flavour. The relatively long cooking time of about 50 minutes can be reduced to 10 minutes if you soak the spelt grains overnight.

❶ Soak the spelt grains overnight in a bowl of water.

❷ Drain the spelt grains thoroughly. Peel the shallots and chop finely. Peel the carrots and cut into thin sticks. Wash and prepare the chillies, cut lengthways, remove the seeds and cut into fine strips.

❸ Heat the olive oil in a large pan and fry the shallots until transparent. Add the spelt grains and fry briefly while stirring. Add the vegetable stock (broth), carrots and chilli. Cover and simmer over a low heat for about 10–15 minutes.

❹ Because the spelt swells up as it absorbs the liquid, it may be necessary to add more liquid. If there is too much liquid left at the end, it can be reduced by boiling it briskly over a high heat without a lid.

❺ Wash the parsley, pat dry, chop the leaves finely and put in the pan. Season the spelt risotto with freshly ground pepper, salt and lemon zest.

Serves 2. About 315 kcal/1320 kJ per serving.
Fat: 7 g • Carbohydrate: 66 g • Protein: 9 g

150 g/5 oz dried unripe spelt grains

2 shallots

4 carrots

1 chilli pepper

1 teaspoon olive oil

400 ml/14 fl oz (1¾ cups) vegetable stock (broth)

1 bunch parsley

grated zest of 1 untreated lemon

freshly ground pepper

sea salt

Farfalle with broccoli

A quick and easy pasta dish with a delicate spicy sauce.

❶ Bring about 1 litre/1¾ pints (4½ cups) water to the boil in a large saucepan and add a little salt.

❷ Wash and prepare the broccoli and divide into small florets. Put the broccoli and pasta in the boiling water and cook until the pasta is ready.

❸ Peel the garlic and put in a mortar with a little sea salt, the chilli powder, peppercorns and anchovy fillets and crush to make a paste. Take 2–3 table-spoons of the pasta-broccoli cooking liquid and stir into the paste.

❹ Drain the pasta and broccoli, arrange on a plate and stir in the spicy sauce. Wash the basil leaves , pat dry and garnish the pasta and broccoli.

Serves 1. About 260 kcal/1090 kJ per serving.
Fat: 5 g • Carbohydrate: 43 g • Protein: 15 g

salt
200 g/7 oz broccoli
50 g/2 oz farfalle
1 clove garlic
coarse sea salt
chilli pepper
a few white peppercorns
2 anchovy fillets (preserved in oil)
some fresh basil leaves

Chinese cabbage roulades with wild rice

A light dish that is easy to digest: Chinese cabbage leaves stuffed with a mixture of minced lamb and wild rice in a tasty paprika sauce. It is worth making double the quantity because these roulades are also very delicious heated up.

125 g/4½ oz mixed wild rice

sea salt

½ head Chinese cabbage

1 bunch chives

2 shallots

1 clove garlic

150 g/5 oz minced (ground) lamb

1 small egg

freshly ground pepper

1 teaspoon cooking oil

60 ml/2 fl oz (4 tablespoons) meat stock (broth)

½ red sweet pepper

1 tablespoon Ajvar (paprika paste, from the can)

❶ Bring 125 ml/4 fl oz (½ cup) salted water to the boil, add the wild rice, cover and simmer over a low heat for about 25 minutes.

❷ Wash and prepare the Chinese cabbage. Cut the central stem from four of the cabbage leaves. Wash the chives and chop finely. Peel the shallots and garlic. Chop 1 shallot and the clove of garlic finely. Mix together the minced lamb , 2 heaped tablespoons rice, half the chopped chives and the egg. Knead into a dough and season generously with salt and pepper

❸ Divide the minced lamb and rice mixture, placing equal amounts on each cabbage leaf. Fold the edges of the leaves over the stuffing and carefully roll up the leaves. Secure with cocktail sticks.

❹ Heat the oil in a non-stick pan and fry the roulades on all sides. Add the meat stock (broth), cover and cook the roulades for about 25 minutes. Remove from the pan and put to one side.

❺ Wash and prepare the pepper and dice. Finely chop the remaining shallot. Add the pepper and shallot to the cooking juices and cook for 3 minutes. Stir in the Ajvar, bring the sauce back to the boil and add the chives.

❻ Arrange the cabbage roulades with the sauce and the remaining rice on two warmed dishes.

Serves 2. About 500 kcal/2100 kJ per serving.
Fat: 22 g • Carbohydrate: 47 g • Protein: 24 g

Pasta stuffed with fish in horseradish sauce

Mustard-flavoured pasta stuffed with a light filling of fish and fresh garden herbs. The delicate sharpness of the horseradish stimulates the appetite and helps digestion.

❶ Stir together the egg, mustard and 1 teaspoon oil. Add the flour and knead to obtain a smooth dough. Cover and leave for 20 minutes.

❷ Rinse the fish, wipe dry with kitchen paper and cut into small cubes. Season the fish with salt and pepper and sprinkle with lime juice. Peel and chop the onion. Heat the remaining oil in a pan and fry the onion until transparent. Add the fish stock (broth) and reduce the liquid. Stir in the crème fraîche and horseradish and season the sauce with salt and pepper. Keep in a warm place.

❸ Bring water to the boil in a small saucepan, blanch the chives for 1 minute, drain and rinse under cold water. Wash the mixed herbs, shake dry and chop finely.

❹ Roll out the pasta dough thinly. Using a cup about 11 cm/4½ in in diameter, cut out 20 circles of dough and brush with egg white. Put some diced fish in the middle of each round piece of dough and fold to make small pouches, tied together with chives.

❺ Bring plenty of water to the boil in a large saucepan and cook the pasta pouches for 10–15 minutes. Remove from the water with a skimming ladle and drain. Serve the pasta pouches with horseradish sauce.

Serves 2. About 410 kcal/1720 kJ per serving.
Fat: 14 g • Carbohydrate: 35 g • Protein: 21 g

1 egg

3 tablespoons strong mustard

2 teaspoons cooking oil

100 g/3½ oz (1 cup) flour

150 g/5 oz sea fish fillet (e.g. rosefish or cod)

herb salt

freshly ground white pepper

juice of ½ lime

1 onion

200 ml/7 fl oz (⅞ cup) fish stock (broth) (from a carton)

1 tablespoon crème fraîche

1 teaspoon horseradish (from the jar)

1 bunch chives

1 bunch mixed fresh herbs (e.g. parsley, chives, chervil, dill)

white of 1 small egg

Spaghetti with tomato sauce

This classic Italian dish is always popular and can be endlessly varied. This sauce is made from fresh tomatoes and red pepper, giving it a distinctive sweetish spicy taste. It can be prepared the day before.

1 clove garlic

1 leek

1 tablespoon olive oil

300 g/10 oz fresh tomatoes

1 red sweet pepper

½ small chilli pepper

200 ml/7 fl oz (⅞ cup) vegetable stock (broth)

salt

250 g/9 oz spaghetti

cayenne pepper

½ teaspoon sugar

1 tablespoon fresh oregano leaves

❶ Peel the garlic and crush. Wash and prepare the leek and cut into thin rounds. Heat the olive oil in a shallow casserole and briefly fry the garlic and leek in it.

❷ Wash the tomatoes, remove the stalk and cut into eight pieces. Wash the pepper, remove the stalk and seeds and cut into thin strips. Add both to the casserole and fry. Wash the chilli, cut lengthways, remove the seeds and chop finely. Add the chilli and vegetable stock (broth) to the pan. Cover and braise for about 15 minutes.

❸ Bring the salted water to the boil in a large saucepan and cook the pasta "al dente" following the instructions on the packet.

❹ Season the tomato and pepper sauce with cayenne pepper, salt and a little sugar. Wash the oregano leaves, dab dry and chop the leaves finely. Boil down to thicken a little more.

❺ Put the spaghetti in two bowls and pour the sauce on top.

Serves 2. About 550 kcal/2310 kJ per serving.
Fat: 7 g • Carbohydrate: 45 g • Protein: 9 g

Rice with pumpkin and mango

An deliciously sweet and spicy dish which is also very nourishing. The mild taste of the pumpkin and fruitiness of the mango combine beautifully with the rice. Rice contains many vital nutrients, especially brown rice. But if brown rice is used, it needs a longer cooking time.

100 g/3½ oz long-grain rice

400 ml/14 fl oz (1¾ cups) vegetable stock (broth)

1 pinch saffron

300 g/10 oz pumpkin

1 tablespoon sunflower oil

1 teaspoon lime juice

freshly ground pepper

some chilli pepper

½ mango

1 tablespoon chopped almonds

❶ Wash the rice. Heat the vegetable stock (broth), add the rice and saffron, cover and simmer over a low heat for about 35–40 minutes. Add more vegetable stock (broth) if necessary – there must always be a little liquid in the pan.

❷ Peel the pumpkin, remove the seeds and soft fibres and cut into cubes. Heat the sunflower oil in a pan and fry the diced pumpkin for a few minutes. Season with lime juice, pepper and chilli powder.

❸ Peel the mango, cut into bite-sized pieces and add to the braised pumpkin. Arrange the rice and pumpkin and mango mixture on two plates and sprinkle with chopped almonds.

Serves 2. About 340 kcal/1430 kJ per serving.

Fat: 10 g • Carbohydrate: 34 g • Protein: 5 g

Lentil and wheat casserole

Lentils play an important part in today's health-conscious cuisine because they contain a lot of fibre and vegetable proteins. The body absorbs proteins better if combined with cereals such as wheat or oats.

1 Peel and finely chop the shallots and garlic . Heat the olive oil in a large casserole and fry the garlic and shallots until transparent.

2 Wash the lentils, add to the pan and fry with the garlic and shallots. Add the vegetable stock (broth) and curry powder. Cover and simmer over a low heat for about 20 minutes.

3 Peel the carrots and cut into slices. Add the carrots and wheat grains to the lentils. Add a little more stock (broth) if necessary. Cook for a further 20 minutes.

4 Season the lentils with salt and freshly ground pepper and stir in the crème fraîche. Wash the thyme leaves, dab dry, chop finely and sprinkle over the casserole.

Serves 2. About 450 kcal/1890 kJ per serving.
Fat: 11 g • Carbohydrate: 64 g • Protein: 20 g

2 shallots
2 cloves garlic
1 tablespoon olive oil
100 g/3½ oz lentils
1 teaspoon curry powder
500 ml/17 fl oz (2¼ cups) vegetable stock (broth)
2 carrots
100 g/3½ oz wheat grains
salt
freshly ground pepper
1 tablespoon crème fraîche
some sprigs of fresh thyme

Indian vegetable curry with almond rice

Lightly fried vegetables served with rice, flavoured with Indian herbs – a culinary and visual delight! Turmeric is one of the main spices used in the preparation of curry powder. It gives food an intense yellow colour and stimulates digestion.

60 g/2 oz dried apricots

½ teaspoon turmeric

125 g/4½ oz easy-cook long-grain rice

1 piece cinnamon stick

1 cardamom seed

sea salt

2 tablespoons flaked (slivered) almonds

3 carrots

½ each red, green and yellow sweet peppers

3 spring onions (scallions)

1 teaspoon groundnut oil

½ teaspoon cumin

½ teaspoon ground coriander

125 ml/4 fl oz (½ cup) vegetable stock (broth)

cayenne pepper

1 tablespoon fresh mint leaves

❶ Cover the apricots with water and bring to the boil. Cover the pan and simmer over a low heat for about 10 minutes. Drain and reserve the cooking liquid. Top up the cooking liquid with water to make 250 ml/8 fl oz (1 cup) of liquid. Add the turmeric, rice, cinnamon and cardamom. Season with salt, cover and simmer over a low heat for 15 minutes. The liquid should be completely absorbed at the end of the cooking time.

❷ Fry the flaked almonds in a non-stick pan without oil until golden yellow. Peel the carrots and cut into slices. Wash and prepare the peppers and cut into thin strips. Wash and prepare the spring onions (scallions) and cut diagonally into rings.

❸ Heat the oil in a pan, add the cumin and coriander and fry briefly. Add the carrots and braise for another 5 minutes. Add the peppers, cover and cook for 5 more minutes. Add the spring onions (scallions) and cook for another 2 minutes. Add the vegetable stock (broth), bring to the boil and season with salt and cayenne pepper.

❹ Dice the apricots. Add to the rice together with the flaked almonds. Chop the mint leaves finely and sprinkle over the vegetables. Arrange the rice and vegetables on two warmed plates.

Serves 2. About 440 kcal/1850 kJ per serving.
Fat: 5 g • Carbohydrate: 74 g • Protein: 7 g

Courgettes (zucchini) with fromage frais and walnut filling

50 g/2 oz shelled walnuts

2 medium courgettes (zucchini)

100 g/3½ oz fromage frais with yoghurt

2 tablespoons low-fat milk (1.5%)

herb salt

freshly ground pepper

1 pinch cayenne pepper

1 tomato

olive oil for the dish

1 tablespoon chopped parsley

Courgettes (zucchini) are a very versatile member of the pumpkin family and they are available throughout the year. Garlic fans can enhance the flavour of the fromage frais by adding a crushed clove of garlic.

❶ Pre-heat the oven to 180°C (350°F), Gas mark 4. Coarsely chop the walnuts. Wash and prepare the courgettes (zucchini) and cut in half lengthways. Scoop out the flesh with a teaspoon, thus creating a hollow. Cut the flesh into small cubes.

❷ Mix the fromage frais and milk and stir to make a smooth mixture. Season with herb salt, pepper and cayenne. Wash the tomatoes, remove the stalks and cut into dice. Add to the fromage frais with the diced courgettes (zucchini) and chopped walnuts. Stir well and check the seasoning again.

❸ Grease an ovenproof dish with olive oil and place the hollowed-out courgette (zucchini) halves in it. Fill them with the fromage frais mixture. Bake in the oven for about 30 minutes. Sprinkle with parsley and serve hot with unleavened bread.

Serves 2. About 270 kcal/1135 kJ per serving.

Fat: 20 g • Carbohydrate: 8 g • Protein: 9 g

Vegetable pancakes (crepes) with herb quark

A light dish which can be prepared with a variety of vegetables. In this recipe, carrots and courgettes (zucchini) are coarsely grated and fried until crisp in a non-stick pan with very little fat. It is delicious served with a home-made herb quark dip.

1 medium courgette (zucchini)

3 large carrots

1 tablespoon lemon juice

freshly ground pepper

½ bunch parsley

1 egg

1 tablespoon oat flakes

1 tablespoon sunflower oil

125 g/4½ oz low-fat quark

1 tablespoon low-fat milk (1.5%)

1 bunch chives

½ small box cress

❶ Wash and prepare the courgette (zucchini), peel the carrots and grate both coarsely. Season with salt and pepper.

❷ Wash the parsley, pat dry, chop the leaves finely and add to the vegetables. Next add the egg and oats and stir well into the vegetables.

❸ Heat the sunflower oil in a non-stick pan. Using a tablespoon, take small portions of the vegetable mixture, put in the pan, press flat and fry on both sides until crisp. Repeat the operation until all the mixture has been used up.

❹ Put the low-fat quark and milk in a small bowl, stir until smooth and season with pepper. Wash and chop the chives and cress, then add to the quark. Arrange the vegetable pancakes with the herb quark on two plates.

Serves 2. About 190 kcal/800 kJ per serving.
Fat: 9 g • Carbohydrate: 9 g • Protein: 10 g

Aubergine (eggplant) gratin

Aubergines (eggplants) absorb a lot of oil while cooking, whether fried, baked or grilled. However, in this recipe they are cooked with other vegetables in a little salted water without any fat, then gratiné with a yoghurt sauce and cheese.

1 aubergine (eggplant)

1 courgette (zucchini)

2 potatoes

100 g/3½ oz broccoli

2 carrots

sea salt

2 onions

1 clove garlic

1 teaspoon olive oil

150 g/5 oz low-fat yoghurt (1.5%)

1 egg

1 tablespoon dried herbs of Provence

freshly ground pepper

30 g/1 oz low-fat hard cheese

❶ Wash and prepare the courgettes and aubergine and cut into slices about 1 cm/⅜ in thick. Peel the potatoes and cut them into slices of the same thickness. Wash the broccoli and divide into florets. Peel the carrots and cut into thick sticks.

❷ Heat 125 ml/4 fl oz (½ cup) water in a large saucepan, season with a little salt and add the vegetables. Cover and simmer over a low heat for about 10 minutes.

❸ Peel the onions and garlic and chop finely. Heat the olive oil in a small pan and fry the onions and garlic until transparent. Drain the aubergine (eggplant) and courgette (zucchini) slices and reserve the cooking liquid. Arrange them with the onion and garlic mixture in alternate layers in the gratin dish.

❹ Pre-heat the oven to 180°C (350°F), Gas mark 4.

❺ Add the egg, 3 tablespoons of the reserved cooking liquid, the herbs of Provence , salt and pepper to the yoghurt, stir well and pour over the vegetables. Grate the cheese and sprinkle on top. Bake the gratin in the oven for about 20–25 minutes.

Serves 2. About 265 kcal/1115 kJ per serving.

Fat: 10 g • Carbohydrate: 25 g • Protein: 13 g

Vegetable kebabs with a spicy dip

You can use almost any vegetable in this recipe, depending on what is available at the time. Cooking the vegetables in the vegetable stock (broth) before grilling them is a useful way of ensuring that the vegetables are cooked enough.

2 onions

2 small courgettes (zucchini)

75 g/3 oz small mushrooms

1 red sweet pepper

125 ml/4 fl oz (½ cup) vegetable stock (broth)

2 teaspoons groundnut oil

freshly ground pepper

juice of 1 lemon

2 metal or wood skewers

for the dip:

5 tablespoons tomato ketchup (catsup)

1 tablespoon low-fat salad cream

1 clove garlic

1 pinch chilli pepper

½ bunch coriander

❶ Peel and halve the onions. Wash and prepare the courgettes (zucchini) and cut into slices 2 cm/¾ in thick . Cut the woody ends off the mushrooms and rub clean with kitchen paper. Cut the pepper into four pieces, remove the stalk and seeds and cut into strips 2 cm/¾ in wide.

❷ Heat the vegetable stock (broth) in a large saucepan, add the vegetables, cover and cook over a medium heat for about 10 minutes.

❸ Pre-heat the oven to 180°C (350°F), Gas mark 4.

❹ Remove the vegetables from the saucepan and drain well. Thread the onion halves, slices of courgette, strips of pepper and whole mushrooms in rotation on long metal or wooden skewers. Brush with oil. Grill for 10–15 minutes. Season with freshly ground pepper and sprinkle with lemon juice.

❺ For the dip, mix the tomato ketchup (catsup) and salad cream together. Peel the garlic and chop finely. Wash the coriander, pat dry and chop the leaves finely. Stir into the sauce. Season the dip with chilli powder and serve with the kebabs.

Serves 2. About 200 kcal/840 kJ per serving.

Fat: 7 g • Carbohydrate: 22 g • Protein: 3 g

3 kohlrabi

3 potatoes

250 ml/8 fl oz (1 cup) vegetable
   stock (broth)

salt

freshly ground pepper

some grated nutmeg

125 g/4½ oz low-fat yoghurt
   (1.5%)

1 egg

1 bunch wild garlic

30 g/1 oz low-fat hard cheese

1 tablespoon sunflower seeds

Kohlrabi gratin
with wild garlic sauce

Wild garlic has a spicy, aromatic flavour and it can be bought fresh in markets in the spring. In other seasons when it is not available it can be replaced by chives.

1 Peel the kohlrabi and potatoes and cut into slices 1 cm/⅜ in thick. Heat the stock (broth) in a saucepan, add the potato and kohlrabi slices, cover and cook for about 15 minutes until ready.

2 Remove the potatoes and kohlrabi from the water, drain well and put in a gratin dish. Season with salt, pepper and freshly grated nutmeg. Wash the wild garlic, chop finely and add together with the egg to the yoghurt. Stir well until smooth and pour over the vegetables.

3 Pre-heat the oven to 180°C (350°F), Gas mark 4.

4 Grate the cheese and sprinkle with the sunflower seeds over the gratin. Bake in the oven for about 10 minutes.

Serves 2. About 310 kcal/1300 kJ per serving.

Fat: 13 g • Carbohydrate: 26 g • Protein: 14 g

Wok-fried vegetables

When eating food prepared in a wok, you can eat to your heart's content because the vegetables contain no fat and only one tablespoon of oil is used to fry all the vegetables. The vegetables are only fried for a short time so they remain crisp and do not lose their vitamins and minerals.

❶ Wash and prepare the pepper and cut into thin strips. Peel the celeriac and carrots and cut into thin sticks. Wash and prepare the spring onions (scallions) and cut into rings. Wash the bean sprouts and drain.

❷ Peel the ginger and garlic and chop finely. Heat the groundnut oil in the wok and briefly fry the ginger and garlic but do not allow to go brown. Add the vegetables and mushrooms and fry for about 3–5 minutes, stirring continuously. The vegetables should remain crisp.

❸ Stir together the vegetable stock (broth), soy sauce and cornflour (corn starch). Pour over the vegetables and bring briefly to the boil. Season with chilli, lemon juice and pepper.

Serves 2. About 170 kcal/710 kJ per serving.
Fat: 7 g • Carbohydrate: 15 g • Protein: 8 g

1 red sweet pepper
½ celeriac root
1 carrot
100 g/3½ oz mushrooms
2 spring onions (scallions)
100 g/3½ oz fresh soy sauce
1 small piece fresh root ginger
1 clove garlic
1 tablespoon groundnut oil
200 ml/7 fl oz (⅞ cup) vegetable stock (broth)
3 tablespoons soy sauce
1 teaspoon cornflour (corn starch)
1 pinch chilli pepper
1 teaspoon lemon juice
freshly ground pepper

Root vegetables with pumpkin seed oil

This salad of fresh root vegetables is ideal as a snack or starter. The root vegetables are grated and served as a salad which will delight all connoisseurs of healthy cuisine. Even the pumpkin seed oil in the dressing is a healthy delicacy because it is rich in trace elements, minerals and vitamins.

❶ Wash, prepare and peel the celeriac, carrots, parsley root and kohlrabi. Using a vegetable grater, grate into thin strips. Put the vegetables in a large bowl.

❷ Mix together the lemon juice, sea salt, multi-coloured pepper and white wine vinegar to make a dressing. Finally, add the pumpkin seed oil and stir carefully with a fork.

❸ Pour the dressing over the raw vegetables and leave to stand for a few minutes. Coarsely chop the cashew nuts and sprinkle over the vegetables. Serve with unleavened bread.

Serves 2. About 114 kcal/480 kJ per serving.
Fat: 7 g • Carbohydrate: 7 g • Protein: 3 g

½ **celery root**

3 **carrots**

1 **parsley root**

½ **kohlrabi**

1 **teaspoon lemon juice**

sea salt

freshly ground multi-coloured
   pepper

1 **tablespoon white wine vinegar**

2 **teaspoons pumpkin seed oil**

1 **tablespoon cashew nuts**

Potato gnocchi with Shiitake mushrooms

Shiitake mushrooms are native to the Far East where they are cultivated on the trunks of oak trees and Shii trees. They have been a much appreciated vegetable in China for centuries. Fresh Shiitake mushrooms are available in shops specialising in oriental food.

400 g/14 oz floury potatoes

sea salt

about 75 g/3 oz (¾ cup) flour

1 small onion

150 g/5 oz Shiitake mushrooms

2 sun-dried tomatoes preserved in oil

75 ml/3 fl oz (⅜ cup) white port

100 ml/3½ fl oz (½ cup) mushroom stock (broth) (from the carton)

herb salt

freshly ground pepper

1 tablespoon butter

1 tablespoon chopped parsley

flour for the work surface

❶ Peel the potatoes, cut into dice and cook in boiling water for about 15 minutes until soft. Drain, push through a potato press or mash, then leave to cool down. Season with salt, add the flour and work into a dough. Leave to rest for 15 minutes.

❷ Meanwhile peel the onions and chop finely. Clean the mushrooms, wipe with kitchen paper and cut into thin slices. Drain the tomatoes and reserve the oil. Cut the tomatoes into thin strips.

❸ Sprinkle flour on the worktop and roll out the dough to make a cylinder about 2.5 cm/1 in in diameter. Cut into pieces about 5 cm/2 in long and make a grooved pattern in them with a fork. Bring a large amount of salted water to the boil, add the gnocchi and cook. They are ready when they rise to the surface.

❹ In the meantime, heat the tomato oil in a second pan and fry the onion until golden yellow. Add the mushrooms, fry briefly and take out of the pan. Add the port and mushroom stock (broth) to the cooking fat and reduce to one-third. Season with herb salt and pepper. Add the butter gradually in small amounts and work into the sauce with a wooden spoon. Add the mushrooms and heat them in the port-flavoured butter.

❺ Drain the gnocchi using a skimming ladle and add the strips of sun-dried tomatoes. Arrange the gnocchi with the mushroom and port wine sauce on two warmed plates and sprinkle with parsley.

Serves 2. About 450 kcal/1890 kJ per serving.
Fat: 12 g • Carbohydrate: 60 g • Protein: 9 g

Chinese fried vegetables with smoked tofu

A light, easy to digest vegetarian dish for brain-workers, rich in minerals, trace elements and vitamins which strengthen the immune system. It can be prepared in 20 minutes and made with a wide range of vegetables and pasta.

❶ Bring plenty of boiling water to the boil, add the buckwheat pasta and cook following the instructions on the packet. Peel the carrots, shallots and garlic. Cut the carrots into small cubes. Chop the onion and garlic finely. Clean the mushrooms and dice small. Rinse the bean sprouts and drain the pasta.

❷ Heat the sesame oil in a deep pan or wok and fry the shallots, garlic, carrots, mushrooms and bean sprouts for 5 minutes, stirring continuously. Cut the smoked tofu into cubes and add to the frying vegetables.

❸ Fry briefly but briskly and season with soy sauce, lime juice, salt and pepper. Sprinkle with chopped coriander just before serving.

Serves 2. About 305 kcal/1280 kJ per serving.
Fat: 11 g • Carbohydrate: 40 g • Protein: 15 g

sea salt

100 g/3½ oz buckwheat pasta

3 large carrots

2 shallots

1 clove garlic

120 g/4 oz oyster mushrooms

50 g/2 oz soy sauce

2 teaspoons sesame oil

100 g/3½ oz smoked tofu

soy sauce

1 teaspoon lime juice

freshly ground pepper

1 tablespoon chopped green coriander

Potato and carrot fricassée

Even fried potatoes can be prepared with very little fat. First they are steamed, then fried with the carrots in a non-stick pan using very little fat.

400 g/14 oz small waxy potatoes

250 g/9 oz carrots

1 onion

1 tablespoon olive oil

1 tablespoon sesame seeds

salt

freshly ground black pepper

some fresh oregano leaves

❶ Clean the potatoes with a brush under the tap and put in a steamer. Peel the carrots and cut into quarters lengthways. Fill the steamer with about 250 ml/8 fl oz (1 cup) water – the water must not reach up to the vegetables – and bring to the boil. Steam the carrots and potatoes for about 20–25 minutes and check if they are cooked enough.

❷ Peel the potatoes and cut into slices. Peel the onions and cut into rings. Heat the olive oil in a large non-stick pan, add the onions and fry. Add the sesame seeds and fry briefly.

❸ Add the carrots and potatoes and fry slowly in the oil, gently turning several times. Season with salt, freshly ground pepper and fresh oregano.

Serves 2. About 260 kcal/1090 kJ per serving.
Fat: 9 g • Carbohydrate: 38 g • Protein: 7 g

Tagliatelle with spinach

A delicious dish which is quick and easy to prepare! It can be served as a main course with a root vegetable salad, but also as an accompaniment to fish and poultry dishes.

sea salt

300 g/10 oz tagliatelle

300 g/10 oz fresh leaf spinach

2 shallots

2 cloves garlic

1 tablespoon pine kernels

2 teaspoons olive oil

100 ml/3½ fl oz (½ cup) low-fat milk (1.5%)

1 teaspoon sauce thickening

herb salt

freshly ground pepper

frisch grated nutmeg

30 g/1 oz(1 cup) grated Pecorino cheese

❶ Bring a large saucepan of salted water to the boil and cook the tagliatelle "al dente" following the instructions on the packet. Remove any damaged leaves and coarse stalks and wash the spinach. Peel the shallots and garlic and chop finely. Fry the pine kernels until golden yellow.

❷ Heat the olive oil in a pan and fry the shallots until golden brown, add the garlic and fry briefly. Add the spinach, let it collapse, cover and cook gently over a low flame for about 3 minutes. Add the milk, bring to the boil and stir in the sauce thickening. Cook until the sauce has thickened, stirring all the time. Season the spinach with herb salt, pepper and a touch of nutmeg.

❸ Drain the tagliatelle and arrange with the spinach on two warmed plates. Sprinkle with the fried pine kernels and Pecorino cheese.

Serves 2. About 745 kcal/3130 kJ per serving.
Fat: 17 g • Carbohydrate: 78 g • Protein: 29 g

Chop Suey

This dish can be varied according to taste and mood, It can be served with chicken, veal or turkey, cut into thin strips, or with crab or prawns. But if you prefer a vegetarian version, you can use seasonal vegetables instead. Whatever the choice, the most important ingredient in chop suey are the bean sprouts which must be served immediately after cooking because they do not remain crisp for long.

❶ Wash and prepare the celery and pepper. Remove the seeds from the pepper. Peel the onions. Rub the mushrooms clean with kitchen paper. Cut all the vegetables into thin strips.

❷ Put the cornflour (corn starch) in a small bowl. Add the soy sauce, sherry and 1 tablespoon water, stir to obtain a smooth mixture and leave to stand briefly.

❸ Heat the sesame oil in a wok or large pan. Add the vegetables and fry for about 5 minutes, stirring continuously. The vegetables must be cooked but still crisp.

❹ Wash the bean sprouts, dab dry and add to the vegetables. Cook for another minute.

❺ Stir the cornflour (corn starch) mixture briefly again and add slowly to the vegetables in the pan. Bring quickly to the boil, stirring continuously. Simmer for 2 more minutes over a low heat while stirring. Season with salt and pepper and serve immediately.

Serves 2. About 175 kcal/735 kJ per serving.
Fat: 9 g • Carbohydrate: 10 g • Protein: 5 g

½ **stick (stalk) celery**

½ **red sweet pepper**

½ **onion**

2 **mushrooms**

1 **teaspoon cornflour (corn starch)**

1 **tablespoon soy sauce**

2 **teaspoons sherry**

1½ **tablespoons sesame oil**

100 g/3½ oz **mung bean sprouts**

75 g/3 oz **soya bean sprouts**

salt

freshly ground pepper

Desserts and pastries

Should you give up cakes and puddings? There's no need to with low-fat cuisine! By using yoghurt instead of cream, you can conjure up delicious light desserts such as for instance the mouthwatering Orange yoghurt ice cream (page 158), the exquisite Bilberry (blueberry) yoghurt (page 150), or Apple strudel with yoghurt vanilla sauce (page 160). Even snacks need not be full of calories as is demonstrated by the tasty Sesame crackers (page 153) or Pumpkin seed croissants (page 163). These are extremely versatile and can be eaten at breakfast, teatime, with friends, or just as a snack.

Zabaglione with blackberries

Zabaglione is an Italian dessert which is made with fresh eggs and white wine. Served with blackberries, it is a light, refreshing pudding which is prepared in no time.

2 fresh egg yolks

2 tablespoons icing (confectioner's) sugar

50 ml/1½ fl oz (3 tablespoons) Marsala

1 teaspoon lemon juice

150 g/5 oz fresh blackberries

❶ Put the egg yolks and icing (confectioner's) sugar in a pudding bowl and whisk with an electric hand-mixer for about 5 minutes on the highest speed until the mixture has become thick and creamy.

❷ Add the Marsala and lemon juice. Heat some water in a large saucepan and keep warm over a low heat. Put the pudding bowl in the water, like a bain marie, and beat the creamy mixture until the mixture becomes very thick. Then put the bowl briefly in cold water to cool the mixture.

❸ Wash the blackberries and arrange on two plates, pour the zabaglione on top and serve immediately.

Serves 2. About 200 kcal/840 kJ per serving.
Fat: 6 g • Carbohydrate: 25 g • Protein: 3 g

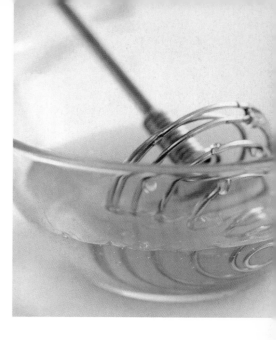

Honey pancakes (crepes)

Sweet pancakes (crepes) can also be low in fat: but it is important to cook them in a non-stick pan so that no oil is needed. The only oil will be in the batter.

❶ Put the spelt flour, buttermilk and thistle oil in a bowl and stir to make a smooth mixture.

❷ Add the two eggs one after the other and beat the batter vigorously. Add the salt and vanilla sugar and stir. Leave the batter to stand for 25 minutes at least and stir again before the next stage.

❸ Heat a non-stick pan and pour in about a quarter of the batter. Cook each pancake (crepe) over a low heat for 2 minutes on each side until golden yellow. Take out of the pan and keep warm.

❹ Spread some honey on the pancakes (crepes) while they are still warm and sprinkle cinnamon according to taste. Roll them up and sprinkle with icing (confectioner's) sugar.

Serves 2. About 250 kcal/1050 kJ per serving.
Fat: 11 g • Carbohydrate: 23 g • Protein: 14 g

60 g/2 oz (½ cup) spelt flour
100 ml/3½ fl oz (½ cup) buttermilk
1 teaspoon thistle oil
2 eggs
1 pinch salt
½ teaspoon vanilla sugar
about 2 tablespoons honey
some cinnamon
icing (confectioner's) sugar

Banana dessert

A healthy diet can also include puddings! This is clearly demonstrated by this mouthwatering banana pudding which is light, easy to digest and contains no fat.

1 banana

1 teaspoon lemon juice

2 teaspoons honey

2 tablespoons oat flakes

❶ Peel the banana and cut in half lengthways. Sprinkle with lemon juice. Pour some honey on a plate and roll the bananas in it so that they are well coated.

❷ Put the oats in a non-stick pan and fry until light brown without adding any fat. Lay the banana halves on the roasted oats and fry for a few minutes on the flat side first. Then turn the banana over very carefully so that the oats do not fall off and fry the other side.

❸ Place the hot bananas on two plates and sprinkle the remaining fried oats on top. Serve immediately.

Serves 2. About 120 kcal/500 kJ per serving.

Fat: 1 g • Carbohydrate: 26 g • Protein: 2 g

Baked pineapple

Pineapple on its own can be eaten in large amounts because it contains a large amount of cleansing substances. But served as dessert, two slices will be enough because the added sugar or honey is turned into fat by the body.

4 slices fresh pineapple (about 1 cm/⅜ in thick)

2 tablespoons acacia honey

2 teaspoons white rum

2 teaspoons coconut milk

❶ Cut the pineapple slices in half, place on a baking sheet covered with aluminium foil and sprinkle rum and acacia honey over them.

❷ Pre-heat the oven to 180°C (350°F), Gas mark 4.

❸ Bake the pineapple in the oven for about 5–8 minutes. Arrange the pineapple pieces on two large plates and sprinkle with coconut milk while still hot.

Serves 2. About 130 kcal/550 kJ per serving.

Fat: 0 g • Carbohydrate: 45 g • Protein: 0 g

Apple in mulled wine

A delicious winter dessert with an exquisite aroma of cloves and cinnamon which is very easy to prepare.

❶ Bring 125 ml/4 fl oz (½ cup) water to the boil in a small saucepan. Add the mulled wine spices and the red wine and simmer over a low heat for about 10 minutes for the flavour to develop. Remove the sachets of spices.

❷ Peel and core the apples and add whole to the wine mixture. Cover and simmer the apples over a low heat for about 15 minutes.

❸ Arrange the braised apples on two plates, add the maple syrup to the mulled wine and reduce briefly over a high heat. Pour the sauce over the apples and serve immediately.

Serves 2. About 145 kcal/610 kJ per serving.
Fat: 0 g • Carbohydrate: 17 g • Protein: 0 g

2 sachets mulled wine spices (including cinnamon and cloves)

125 ml/4 fl oz (½ cup) red wine

2 apples

2 teaspoons maple syrup

Figs in red wine and blackberry sauce

A deliciously fruity pudding inspired by Mediterranean cuisine and a perfect conclusion to a light meal.

① Wash the blackberries and put a few aside as a garnish. Purée the rest with a hand-mixer. Rub the purée through a fine sieve into a saucepan.

② Add the red wine and heat up slowly. Mix the starch with 1 teaspoon water and stir until smooth. Add to the fruit purée and stir in carefully, making sure that there are no lumps. Bring briefly to the boil and sweeten with a tablespoon of honey.

③ Wash and prepare the figs and cut into slices. Arrange the fruit on two dessert plates and pour the hot red wine and blackberry sauce over it. Garnish with blackberries.

Serves 2. About 124 kcal/520 kJ per serving.
Fat: 0 g • Carbohydrate: 19 g • Protein: 1 g

125 g/4½ oz blackberries

125 ml/4 fl oz (½ cup) red wine

½ teaspoon cornflour (corn starch)

1 tablespoon honey

3 fresh figs

Raspberry sorbet

This mouth-watering raspberry sorbet is completely fat-free and it makes a perfect pudding for a warm summer's day.

100 g/3½ oz raspberries

1 tablespoon lemon juice

1 tablespoon honey

125 ml/4 fl oz (½ cup) Prosecco

1 teaspoon raspberry liqueur

some leaves of lemon balm

❶ Wash and prepare the raspberries. Purée the fruit and rub it through a fine sieve into a small freezer-proof container.

❷ Mix the lemon juice, honey, Prosecco and raspberry liqueur together. Put the fruit purée in the freezer and leave it for 3 hours to set. During the first hour, stir with a small whisk every 15 minutes, then repeat every 30 minutes.

❸ Put the raspberry sorbet in chilled glasses, garnish with lemon balm and serve immediately.

Serves 2. About 115 kcal/480 kJ per serving.
Fat: 0 g • Carbohydrate: 12 g • Protein: 0 g

Bilberry (blueberry) yoghurt

Yoghurt is an ideal base for light puddings and combines beautifully with many fruits. If guests arrive unexpectedly, this delicious dish can prepared in just a few minutes.

100 g/3½ oz bilberries (blueberries)

2 teaspoons maple syrup

1 pinch cinnamon

250 g/9 oz low-fat yoghurt (1.5%)

❶ Wash the bilberries (blueberries) and put a few to one side. Put the rest in a tall container with the maple syrup and a pinch of cinnamon. Purée with a hand-held mixer.

❷ Using a whisk, stir the yoghurt into the bilberry (blueberry) purée. Pour into two small bowls and garnish with the reserved bilberries (blueberries).

Serves 2. About 110 kcal/460 kJ per serving.

Fat: 1 g • Carbohydrate: 16 g • Protein: 4 g

Melon and orange salad

Melons contain a lot of water and very little fructose, which makes them ideal as a refreshing dessert. They make a delicious fruit salad when combined with oranges.

¼ watermelon

1 orange

1 teaspoon orange liqueur

½ teaspoon cinnamon

1 teaspoon honey

1 tablespoon lemon juice

1 tablespoon walnuts

❶ Peel the watermelon, remove the seeds and cut the flesh into small cubes. Peel the orange and cut into segments. Cut the orange segments in half and put in a bowl with the diced melon.

❷ Mix the orange liqueur, cinnamon, honey and lemon juice together. Pour it over the fruit salad and stir well. Put in a cool place and leave to stand for about 30 minutes. Coarsely chop the walnuts and sprinkle over the melon and orange salad.

Serves 2. About 180 kcal/760 kJ per serving.

Fat: 6 g • Carbohydrate: 19 g • Protein: 2 g

Blackberry tartlets

These tartlets are quick and easy to make and can be prepared with any kind of fruit. Wholemeal (wholewheat) spelt flour gives the pastry a strong nutty flavour.

❶ Put the flour, lemon juice and zest, egg yolk, salt, sugar and softened butter in a mixing bowl and knead into a smooth dough. Leave to rest for 30 minutes.

❷ Pre-heat the oven to 180°C (350°F), Gas mark 4.

❸ Grease the tartlet moulds (about 10 cm/4 in in diameter) with a little butter, roll out the dough to a thickness of 0.5 cm/³⁄₁₆ in and line the moulds with it. Bake blind in the oven for 15 minutes.

❹ Remove the tartlets from the oven, leave to cool down, and arrange the blackberries in them. Sprinkle with cinnamon and sugar.

Serves 2. About 290 kcal/1830 kJ per serving.
Fat: 25 g • Carbohydrate: 45 g • Protein: 6 g

75 g/3 oz (¾ cup) spelt flour
zest and juice of 1 untreated lemon
1 egg yolk
1 pinch salt
30 g/1 oz (1 tablespoon) sugar
50 g/2 oz (4 tablespoons) butter
about 150 g/5 oz blackberries
1 teaspoon sugar
½ teaspoon cinnamon
some butter for the moulds

Sesame crackers

Ideal for a nibble in between meals, these crisp little sesame crackers are quick and easy to make. They will keep several days if stored in a tin or plastic box.

❶ Put the spelt flakes and wheat grains in a mixing bowl, add about 400 ml/14 fl oz (1¾ cups) water and stir to make a semi-liquid dough. Leave to stand for 1 hour.

❷ Pre-heat the oven to 180°C (350°F), Gas mark 4.

❸ Stir the sesame seeds and salt into the dough. Grease the baking sheet with a little oil and spread out the dough on it. Bake in the oven for about 15 minutes.

❹ Remove the dough from the oven and, using a sharp knife, cut a triangular or diamond-shaped pattern in the dough.

❺ Replace on the baking sheet and bake for a further 15–20 minutes until crisp. Remove from the oven, leave to cool and break into triangles or diamond shapes.

Whole baking sheet about 1195 kcal/5020 kJ.
Fat: 42 g • Carbohydrate: 170 g • Protein: 46 g

125 g/4½ oz spelt flakes
125 g/4½ oz fine wheat grains
60 g/2 oz sesame seeds
1 teaspoon sea salt
1 teaspoon olive oil

Fruit salad with lemon dressing

The fruit can be chosen according to taste and season. The lemon dressing adds a delicate sharp touch to the salad and helps prevent the fruit from going brown too quickly.

1 banana

1 apricot

1 piece honeydew melon (about 200 g/7 oz)

1 clementine

1 tablespoon lemon juice

1 tablespoon maple syrup

1 tablespoon crème fraîche

❶ Peel the banana and cut into slices, peel the apricot, halve it, remove the stone (pit) and cut into quarters. Peel the honeydew melon, remove the seeds and cut into small pieces. Peel the clementines and divide into segments. Arrange the fruit in two bowls.

❷ Make the sauce with the lemon juice, maple syrup and crème fraîche and pour over the fruit.

Serves 2. About 165 kcal/690 kJ per serving.
Fat: 3 g • Carbohydrate: 29 g • Protein: 1 g

Peach gratin

This deliciously fragrant peach gratin will take about 40 minutes to prepare but the result is well worth it.

❶ Blanch the peaches briefly in hot water and peel. Cut the flesh in slices off the stone (pit). Sprinkle orange juice over the fruit.

❷ Separate the egg and beat the egg yolk with 1 tablespoon of the icing (confectioner's) sugar until foamy. Stir in the quark. Beat the egg white into stiff peaks with the rest of the icing (confectioner's) sugar and a pinch of salt. Add the stiffly beaten egg white to the quark mixture.

❸ Pre-heat the oven to 200°C (400°F), Gas mark 6.

❹ Grease a small ovenproof gratin dish with butter and arrange the peach slices in it. Sprinkle chopped almonds over them. Pour the quark mixture over all and bake in the oven for about 15 minutes. Serve hot.

Serves 2. About 255 kcal/1070 kJ per serving.
Fat: 6 g • Carbohydrate: 33 g • Protein: 14 g

2 peaches
1 tablespoon orange juice
1 egg
2 tablespoons icing
   (confectioner's) sugar
125 g/4½ oz low-fat quark
1 pinch salt
½ teaspoon butter
1 teaspoon chopped almonds

Lemon jelly with mango

The refreshing sharp taste of the jelly and the fruity sweetness of the mango make an exciting contrast. In addition, this exquisite dessert has the advantage of containing no fat at all.

zest and juice of 2 untreated lemons

100 ml/3½ fl oz (½ cup) unsweetened grapefruit juice

50 ml/1½ fl oz (3 tablespoons) orange juice

1 teaspoon acacia honey

½ sachet powdered gelatine

1 mango

❶ Put the lemon juice and zest in a small saucepan, add the grapefruit juice, the orange juice and the acacia honey and heat slowly.

❷ In the meantime, put the powdered gelatine in 3 tablespoons of water and leave to soak for 10 minutes. Add the gelatine to the hot (but not boiling) fruit juice and dissolve, stirring continuously.

❸ Remove the saucepan from the heat and let the liquid cool down a little. Pour the lemon jelly into two glass bowls and put in the refrigerator for 3 hours.

❹ Peel the mango just before serving, cut the flesh from the stone (pit) and cut into bite-sized pieces. Garnish the chilled jelly with the pieces of mango.

Serves 2. About 80 kcal/335 kJ per serving.

Fat: 0 g • Carbohydrate: 12 g • Protein: 3 g

Orange yoghurt ice cream

You can make this delicious ice cream yourself and reduce the calories at the same time, because yoghurt is used instead of cream. This gives the dish a delicate, slightly sharp taste.

juice and grated zest of 2 untreated oranges

1 tablespoon acacia honey

250 g/9 oz fat-free yoghurt

2 tablespoons grated chocolate

❶ Mix the orange juice, orange zest and acacia honey. Add the yoghurt and stir thoroughly with a whisk.

❷ Pour the orange-yoghurt mixture into a freezer-proof container and put in the freezer compartment for about 3 hours.

❸ Using 2 tablespoons, arrange portions of the yoghurt ice cream on two plates. Sprinkle with grated chocolate.

Serves 2. About 95 kcal/400 kJ per serving.
Fat: 3 g • Carbohydrate: 13 g • Protein: 4 g

Strawberries in bilberry (blueberry) sauce

An exquisite delicacy: fresh strawberries served in a delicious bilberry (blueberry) sauce – with no fat at all!

125 g/4½ oz (1 cup) bilberries (blueberries)

1 tablespoon maple syrup

2 teaspoons port

200 g/7 oz (1¼ cups) strawberries

a little icing (confectioner's) sugar

fresh mint leaves

❶ Put the bilberries (blueberries) in a saucepan. Add the maple syrup and port. Bring to the boil while stirring and simmer over a low heat for 5 minutes until the berries burst open, resulting in a thick sauce-like mixture.

❷ Wash the strawberries, hull (shuck) and cut the fruit in half. Arrange them on two pudding plates and pour the sauce over while still hot. Sprinkle icing (confectioner's) sugar on top and garnish with mint leaves.

Serves 2. About 115 kcal/480 kJ per serving.
Fat: 0 g • Carbohydrate: 15 g • Protein: 1 g

2 eggs

50 g/2 oz (scant ½ cup) icing
(confectioners) sugar

1 pinch salt

40 g/1½ oz (scant ½ cup) coarse
wholemeal (wholewheat) flour

½ teaspoon baking powder

2 tablespoons vanilla sugar

2 bananas

2 teaspoons low-fat quark

1 teaspoon semi-skimmed milk
(1.5 %)

Banana omelette

A banana omelette is a delicious way of ending a light meal and it also makes a delicious sweet snack. It is best eaten as soon as it has been prepared. Naturally the omelette may also be filled with other fruit.

❶ Pre-heat the oven to 180°C (350°F), Gas mark 4.

❷ Separate the eggs. Put the egg yolks in a bowl and beat with half the icing (confectioner's) sugar and two tablespoons of warm water to make a pale yellow foamy mixture. Add a pinch of salt to the egg whites and beat until stiff, then add the remaining sugar.

❸ Add the beaten egg whites, flour and baking powder to the egg yolk mixture and fold in carefully. Line a baking sheet with greaseproof (waxed) paper. Put 4 balls of the mixture on the paper, leaving room between them, and flatten the tops slightly. Bake the omelettes in the oven for about 10–15 minutes until light brown.

❹ Sprinkle vanilla sugar on a clean tea towel and turn the hot omelettes upside down onto it. Remove the greaseproof (waxed) paper.

❺ Peel the bananas and cut into slices. Mix the milk and quark and add to the banana slices. Fill the omelettes with the banana-quark mixture and serve immediately.

Serves 2. About 510 kcal/2140 kJ per serving.
Fat: 6 g • Carbohydrate: 87 g • Protein: 11 g

Apple strudel with yoghurt vanilla sauce

The classic apple strudel becomes a delicious calorie-reduced pudding when served with a low-calorie yoghurt sauce.

100 g/3½ oz (1 cup) finely ground wholemeal (whole wheat) flour

1 pinch salt

2–3 tablespoons water

2 tablespoons thistle oil

200 g/7 oz apple

1 tablespoon lemon juice

1 teaspoon sugar

1 teaspoon cinnamon

125 g/4½ oz low-fat yoghurt (1.5%)

2 tablespoons low-fat milk (1.5%)

1 teaspoon vanilla sugar

❶ Mix the wholemeal (wholewheat) flour with salt, water and oil and work into a smooth dough. Put in the refrigerator for 30 minutes.

❷ Peel the apples, cut into quarters, remove the core and cut into small pieces. Sprinkle lemon juice on top. Stir in the sugar and cinnamon.

❸ Roll out the dough into a thin rectangle on a floured work surface. Put the apple filling on the dough and roll it up to make a strudel. Fold in the ends.

❹ Pre-heat the oven to 200 °C (400 °F), Gas mark 6.

❺ Line a baking sheet with greaseproof (waxed) paper and put the strudel on it. Bake in the oven for about 35–40 minutes.

❻ Stir the milk and vanilla sugar into the yoghurt. Cut the strudel into thick slices and serve with the yoghurt sauce.

Serves 2. About 380 kcal/1595 kJ per serving.

Fat: 15 g • Carbohydrate: 50 g • Protein: 8 g

Mango granita

This refreshingly fruity summer pudding is a granita, a light, semi-frozen pudding from Italy which can be prepared with a wide range of fruits or coffee. The refined tangy flavour is enhanced by the addition of sparkling wine.

❶ Peel the mango, cut the flesh away from the stone (pit) and chop into small pieces.

❷ Put the pieces of fruit, sparkling wine and orange juice in a tall container and make a smooth purée using a hand-mixer.

❸ Put the puréed fruit in a flat freezer tray and put in the freezer. As soon as the fruit begins to freeze, remove the purée from the container, put it in a mixing bowl and stir briskly.

❹ Beat the egg whites into stiff peaks, add the icing (confectioner's) sugar and carefully fold into the fruit purée. Put the mixture back in the freezer compartment until the fruit purée is completely frozen.

Serves 2. About 111 kcal/470 kJ per serving.
Fat: 0 g • Carbohydrate: 15 g • Protein: 3 g

1 ripe mango

75 ml/3 fl oz (⅜ cup) sparkling white wine

75 ml/3 fl oz (⅜ cup) orange juice

1 egg white

1 teaspoon icing (confectioner's) sugar

Grapefruit cream

This pudding is prepared with low-fat quark. It is the gelatine which gives the pudding its consistency, which is why the pudding must be chilled for a few hours.

1 Halve the grapefruit and squeeze out the juice. Stir the powdered gelatine into 3 tablespoons of grapefruit juice and leave to soak for 10 minutes.

2 Beat the egg whites stiff and add the icing (confectioner's) sugar. Mix together the quark and crème fraîche and add the rest of the grapefruit juice. Heat the gelatine until it is completely dissolved, stirring continuously. Leave to cool slightly and add to the quark mixture.

3 Finally, fold in the stiffly beaten eggs. Put the grapefruit cream in two bowls and put in the refrigerator for about 3 hours.

Serves 2. About 235 kcal/990 kJ per serving.

Fat: 6 g • Carbohydrate: 29 g • Protein: 20 g

1 pink grapefruit

½ sachet powdered gelatine

2 egg whites

3 tablespoons icing (confectioner's) sugar

200 g/7 oz low-fat quark

1 tablespoon crème fraîche

Pumpkin seed croissant

These delicious croissants are ideal for a tasty breakfast or teatime snack. They are made from yeast dough with a little honey but hardly any fat.

❶ Put the wholemeal (wholewheat) wheat, oat flakes and pumpkin seeds in a bowl and make a well in the centre. Dissolve the honey and yeast in about 125 ml/4 fl oz (½ cup) lukewarm water and pour into the central well and stir in a little flour from the sides.

❷ Add the salt and 1 egg yolk along the edge of the flour. Work all the ingredients to a smooth dough; if the dough is too stiff, add a little lukewarm water. Cover the dough with a cloth and stand in warm place for 20 minutes.

❸ Pre-heat the oven to 200°C (400°F), Gas mark 6.

❹ Knead the dough briefly once more, shape into a cylinder and cut into 6 pieces. Shape each piece into a croissant. Line a baking sheet with some greaseproof (waxed) paper and put the croissants on it. Brush the top of the croissants with the second egg yolk and bake in the oven for about 20–25 minutes until golden yellow.

Serves 2. Each croissant about 185 kcal/780 kJ.

Fat: 6 g • Carbohydrate: 26 g • Protein: 9 g

150 g/6 oz (1½ cups) fine wholemeal (wholewheat) flour

100 g/3½ oz oat flakes

1 tablespoon pumpkin seeds

20 g/¾ oz yeast

1 teaspoon honey

sea salt

2 egg yolks

Buckwheat croissants

A savoury croissant which is quick and easy to prepare. It contains very little fat and is delicious with a glass of wine. These savoury croissants are made from buckwheat which has a delicate nutty flavour.

150 g/6 oz (1½ cups) buckwheat flour

150 g/6 oz (1½ cups) fine wholemeal (wholewheat) flour

2 tablespoons sunflower oil

1 pinch ground cardamom

1 teaspoon sea salt

1 egg yolk

some sesame seeds

❶ Put the buckwheat and wholemeal (wholewheat) flour, sunflower oil, cardamom, salt and about 200 ml/7 fl oz (⅞ cup) water in a bowl and work into a smooth dough. Wrap in the aluminium foil and put in the refrigerator for about 30 minutes.

❷ Knead the dough once more, shape into a cylinder of about 5 cm/2 in in diameter and cut into pieces. Shape these pieces into croissants. Line a baking-sheet with grease-proof paper and put the croissants on it.

❸ Heat the oven to 180°C (350°F), Gas mark 4.

❹ Mix the egg yolk with 1 teaspoon water and brush the croissants with this mixture. Sprinkle sesame on top. Bake in the oven for about 10–15 minutes.

Whole baking sheet: about 1410 kcal/5920 kJ.

Fat: 47 g • Carbohydrate: 212 g • Protein: 37 g

Strawberry quark

A pudding which can be conjured up in no time at all. Other summer fruit can be used instead of strawberries.

250 g/9 oz fresh strawberries

200 g/7 oz low-fat quark

2 tablespoons low-fat milk (1.5%)

1 tablespoon maple syrup

1 pinch grated untreated orange zest

2 tablespoons oat flakes

❶ Wash the strawberries and remove the stalks. Cut them in half and arrange in two bowls.

❷ Mix the milk and quark together until you obtain a smooth mixture and sweeten to taste with the maple syrup and grated orange zest. Pour this mixture over the strawberries.

❸ Fry the oats in a non-stick pan without fat until pale brown and sprinkle over the strawberry quark.

Serves 2. About 180 kcal/760 kJ per serving.
Fat: 1 g • Carbohydrate: 23 g • Protein: 15 g

Quark delight with almonds

The fried almonds give this quark pudding a delicate nutty flavour. In order to keep the calories down, it is important to use low-fat quark and unsweetened fruit.

250 g/9 oz low-fat quark

2 tablespoons low-fat milk (1.5%)

1 tablespoon maple syrup

2 nectarines

1 tablespoon almonds

❶ Mix together the milk and maple syrup. Put the quark into two pudding bowls.

❷ Peel the nectarines, cut in half, remove the stone (pit) and cut into slices. Arrange the nectarine slices on the quark.

❸ Coarsely chop the almonds, fry in a pan without fat and sprinkle over the quark and nectarine slices.

Serves 2. About 215 kcal/900 kJ per serving.
Fat: 4 g • Carbohydrate: 22 g • Protein: 18 g

Pear compote

This mouth-watering pudding is made from pears cooked in an aromatic liquid and garnished with ricotta and flaked almonds.

1 Put the cinnamon stick, cloves, lemon zest and maple syrup in a saucepan with 4 tablespoons water and bring to the boil. Remove from the heat and allow to stand for a few seconds.

2 Peel the pears, cut into quarters, remove the core and add to the mixture. Cover and simmer the pears for about 5–8 minutes.

3 Remove the pears from the liquid and place them still lukewarm on two plates. Garnish each with a tablespoon of ricotta and sprinkle with flaked almonds.

Serves 2. About 120 kcal/500 kJ per serving.
Fat: 3 g • Carbohydrate: 12 g • Protein: 2 g

1 cinnamon stick

2 cloves

1 small piece untreated lemon zest

1 teaspoon maple syrup

2 pears

2 tablespoons ricotta cheese

1 teaspoon flaked (slivered) almonds

Drinks

Low-fat cuisine also includes drinks. There are thirst-quenchers full of vitamins such as the Cucumber and red pepper drink (page 173). Pear and banana shake (page 176) makes a low-calorie snack, while delicious non-alcoholic drinks such as the Citrus fruit cocktail (page 174) and Spiced tomato cocktail (page 182) will complete your well-balanced diet.

Exotic fruit drink

This fruit drink made from papaya and mango is a delicious summer drink and does not contain any fat at all. Like other fruit juices, it can also be diluted to taste with mineral water.

❶ Peel the papaya and mango, remove the stone (pit) and cut the flesh into small cubes.

❷ Cut the orange in half and squeeze the juice . Pour the orange juice, cubed papaya and mango into the liquidizer and purée.

❸ Season the fruit drink with a pinch of cinnamon, dilute to taste with mineral water and pour into a large glass.

Makes 1 glass. About 143 kcal/600 kJ per glass.
Fat: 0 g • Carbohydrate: 29 g • Protein: 2 g

½ **papaya**
½ **mango**
1 orange
pinch cinnamon
sparkling mineral water

Mango buttermilk

This is a sweet, fruity drink with only a very small amount of fat. You can make this delicious drink whenever you like because mangos are now available almost all year round.

1 ripe mango

½ banana

300 ml/10 fl oz (1¼ cups) buttermilk

1 teaspoon orange juice

1 pinch ground ginger

❶ Peel the mangos and banana. Remove the stone (pit) and cut the mango into slices, putting two slices aside for the garnish. Put the diced mango and banana in the liquidizer and purée.

❷ Add the puréed fruit to the buttermilk and stir well. Season with orange juice and ground ginger and pour into a large glass. Garnish with the slices of mango.

Makes 1 glass. About 310 kcal/1300 kJ per glass.
Fat: 3 g • Carbohydrate: 54 g • Protein: 12 g

Cucumber and red pepper drink

It need not always be lemonade – a vegetable drink like this one is extremely refreshing and very thirst-quenching on a hot summer's day.

❶ Peel the cucumber, remove the seeds and cut into cubes. Wash the pepper, remove the stalk and seeds, and chop. Put the vegetables in the liquidizer, then rub through a fine sieve.

❷ Peel the garlic, press it through a garlic press and add to the puréed vegetables. Stir in the yoghurt – and mineral water to taste – and whisk vigorously. Season the drink with sea salt, freshly ground pepper and finely chopped dill.

Makes 1 glass. About 115 kcal/480 kJ per glass.

Fat: 0 g • Carbohydrate: 15 g • Protein: 6 g

200 g/7 oz cucumber

1 red sweet pepper

½ clove garlic

100 g/3½ oz low-fat yoghurt (1.5%)

sparkling mineral water

sea salt

freshly ground pepper

1 teaspoon chopped dill

Carrot and orange drink

Vegetable and fruit drinks are truly invigorating and very delicious. They are full of important vitamins and minerals and contain hardly any fat. For people with little time, they can also be mixed from ready-made juices (without added sugar!), available in health food shops.

1 orange
150 ml/5 fl oz (⅝ cup) carrot juice
pinch cinnamon
1 teaspoon honey
½ teaspoon cream

❶ Peel the orange, cut in half, cut off one slice and put to one side. Squeeze the rest of the orange.

❷ Mix the orange juice with the carrot juice, stir in the cream and season with a pinch of cinnamon and honey. Pour into a large glass and garnish with the slice of orange.

Makes 1 glass. About 160 kcal/670 kJ per glass.
Fat: 3 g • Carbohydrate: 29 g • Protein: 1 g

Citrus fruit cocktail

A spicy, refreshing summer drink with no fat at all made with freshly squeezed grapefruit and orange mixed with pineapple juice.

juice of 1 grapefruit
juice of 1 orange
200 ml/7 fl oz (⅞ cup)
    unsweetened pineapple juice
pinch ground ginger
ice cubes
½ carambola (star fruit)

❶ Mix together the freshly squeezed orange and grapefruit juice and add the pineapple juice. Season with freshly ground ginger and pour into a glass with ice cubes.

❷ Cut the carambola (star fruit) into slices, make a notch in each slice and slip onto the edge of the glass as decoration.

Makes 1 glass. About 180 kcal/760 kJ per glass.
Fat: 0 g • Carbohydrate: 41 g • Protein: 0 g

Pear and banana shake

This milk shake is like a small meal in itself because the bananas and milk contain many important nutrients. It is therefore an amazing source of energy.

1 banana

1 pear

250 ml/8 fl oz (1 cup) low-fat milk (1.5%)

1 teaspoon grated chocolate

❶ Peel the bananas and pears. Remove the core from the pear. Cut the pear and banana into pieces and purée with the milk in the liquidizer. Pour the milk shake into a large glass and sprinkle with grated chocolate.

Makes 1 glass. About 300 kcal/1260 kJ per glass.
Fat: 6 g • Carbohydrate: 50 g • Protein: 7 g

Grapefruit and coconut juice

Citrus fruits are rich in vitamin C which protects the body against colds. Grapefruit juice is extremely refreshing and can be made in no time at all all the year round.

1 grapefruit

juice of ½ lime

1 teaspoon honey

2 tablespoons coconut milk

1 teaspoon grated coconut

❶ Halve the grapefruit and squeeze the juice. Mix the grapefruit juice with the juice of half a lime, sweeten with honey and sprinkle with grated coconut.

Makes 1 glass. About 115 kcal/480 kJ per glass.
Fat: 0 g • Carbohydrate: 17 g • Protein: 0 g

Pepper and celery drink

You can prepare vegetable juices yourself if you have a juicer. But naturally it is quicker with ready-made juices available in health food shops. The drink is chilled with iced whey cubes which you can make yourself in the freezer.

100 ml/3½ fl oz (½ cup) whey

200 ml/7 fl oz (⅞ cup) celery juice

100 ml/3½ fl oz (½ cup) red pepper juice

1 pinch chilli pepper

grated nutmeg

½ bunch chives

❶ Pour the whey into an ice-cube tray and put in the freezer.

❷ Stir the celery and red pepper juice together. Season with chilli powder and a pinch of grated nutmeg.

❸ Wash the chives, pat dry and chop finely. Remove the tray with iced whey cubes, put them in a large glass, pour in the juice and sprinkle with the chopped chives.

Makes 1 glass. About 110 kcal/460 kJ per glass.

Fat: 0 g • Carbohydrate: 21 g • Protein: 3 g

Peach and kiwi fruit milk shake

You should choose very ripe fruit to make this milk shake. This will make it much easier when you purée them. Instead of a peach, apricot or nectarine can also be used.

❶ Peel the peach and kiwi fruit, remove the peach stone (pit) and cut both fruits into eight pieces. Put in a tall container, add a pinch of vanilla sugar and a tablespoon of sour milk, and purée with a hand-held electric mixer.

❷ Add the puréed fruit to the rest of the sour milk and stir well. If the milk-shake is too thick, add some more sour milk. Pour into a tall glass and sprinkle with chopped hazelnuts.

Makes 1 glass. About 265 kcal/1110 kJ per glass.
Fat: 7 g • Carbohydrate: 31 g • Protein: 11 g

1 peach
1 kiwi fruit
1 pinch vanilla sugar
125 ml/4 fl oz (½ cup) low-fat sour milk
some skimmed milk
1 teaspoon chopped hazelnuts

Cinnamon and honey flavoured cocoa

It need not always be coffee or tea – cinnamon is a very pleasant alternative flavour for that time of the day when you need a lift. Also, being prepared with low-fat milk, it is very low in calories.

200 ml/7 fl oz (⅞ cup) low-fat milk (1.5%)

1 teaspoon cocoa powder

1 pinch cinnamon

1 pinch ground cardamom

1 teaspoon honey

1 teaspoon chocolate flakes

❶ Heat up the milk, add the cocoa powder and stir until it is dissolved. Bring the cocoa briefly to the boil.

❷ Season the cocoa with a pinch of cinnamon and cardamom and sweeten with honey to taste. Pour the hot cocoa into a mug and garnish with chocolate flakes.

Makes 1 glass. About 155 kcal/480 kJ per glass.

Fat: 5 g • Carbohydrate: 20 g • Protein: 8 g

Hazelnut milk drink

Nuts are relatively high in fat which is why they should be used sparingly in low-fat cuisine. But their delicate flavour still comes through, even in small amounts, especially when freshly ground.

1 tablespoon shelled hazelnuts

100 g/3½ oz low-fat yoghurt (1.5%)

200 ml/7 fl oz (⅞ cup) low-fat milk

1 teaspoon honey

½ teaspoon vanilla sugar

❶ Grind the hazelnuts finely. Put in a tall container, add the yoghurt and stir vigorously with a small whisk.

❷ Sweeten the milk-shake to taste with honey and vanilla sugar.

Makes 1 glass. About 245 kcal/1030 kJ per glass.

Fat: 9 g • Carbohydrate: 25 g • Protein: 11 g

Spiced tomato cocktail

Hot spices such as chilli powder have stimulating properties, so just a pinch will turn this tomato juice into quite an invigorating drink that will give you a lift between meals.

200 g/7 oz tomatoes
1 teaspoon chives
1 tablespoon low-fat sour milk
1 pinch chilli pepper
lemon juice
sparkling mineral water

❶ Wash the tomatoes, remove the stalks, chop into pieces, purée and rub through a fine sieve.

❷ Add the chopped chives and stir in the sour milk. Season with chilli powder and lemon juice. Dilute with mineral water according to taste.

Makes 1 glass. About 55 kcal/231 kJ per glass.
Fat: 0 g • Carbohydrate: 5 g • Protein: 0 g

Nectarine shake with wheat germ

This milk-shake is made with buttermilk and enriched with wheat germ. As a result, it is deliciously refreshing with a slightly sour taste as well as very nourishing.

2 nectarines
300 ml/10 fl oz (1¼ cups) buttermilk
1 teaspoon maple syrup
1 tablespoon wheat germ

❶ Peel the nectarines, cut them in half, remove the stone (pit) and purée in the liquidizer.

❷ Add the buttermilk and stir well. Sweeten the nectarine shake with maple syrup, pour into a tall glass and sprinkle wheat germ on top.

Makes 1 glass. About 245 kcal/1030 kJ per glass.
Fat: 2 g • Carbohydrate: 37 g • Protein: 15 g

Avocado and kefir drink

A creamy mild drink, made from very healthy ingredients. Avocados are full of healthy unsaturated fatty acids, while the slightly tangy kefir with its lactic acid bacteria activates the body's metabolism.

1 Scoop out the flesh of the avocado pear with a spoon. Sprinkle with lemon juice and purée in the liquidizer.

2 Add the kefir and stir well. Season the avocado and kefir drink with freshly ground pepper. Pour into a glass and sprinkle the chopped chives on top.

Makes 1 glass. About 295 kcal/1240 kJ per glass.

Fat: 25 g • Carbohydrate: 5 g • Protein: 8 g

½ **ripe avocado**
1 teaspoon lemon juice
150 ml/5 fl oz (⅝ cup) kefir
freshly ground white pepper
1 teaspoon chives

Strawberry buttermilk drink

A heavenly drink which can be enjoyed every day in the strawberry season without any feeling of remorse. Strawberries contain no fat, while buttermilk is rich in protein and lecithin.

200 g/7 oz strawberries

1 tablespoon maple syrup

½ teaspoon grated untreated lemon zest

125 ml/4 fl oz (½ cup) buttermilk

1 teaspoon grated coconut

a few leaves lemon balm

❶ Wash the strawberries. Remove the stalks and any blemishes. Purée with the maple syrup and grated lemon zest. Mix the strawberry purée and buttermilk together.

❷ Pour the strawberry buttermilk drink into a tall glass, sprinkle with grated coconut and garnish with lemon balm.

Makes 1 glass. About 112 kcal/470 kJ per glass.

Fat: 1 g • Carbohydrate: 14 g • Protein: 9 g

Watermelon drink

A refreshing drink, ideal for a hot summer's day. This watermelon shake contains hardly any calories and can be diluted with mineral water, or on special occasions, with Prosecco or other sparkling white wine.

1 piece watermelon (about 200 g/7 oz)

ground ginger

½ teaspoon vanilla sugar

1 teaspoon lemon juice

125 ml/4 fl oz (½ cup) sparkling mineral water or Prosecco (or other sparkling white wine)

a few mint leaves

1 Peel the watermelon and remove the seeds, cut into cubes and put in a tall mixing bowl. Purée the watermelon with a hand-held electric mixer. Season with a pinch of ground ginger, a little vanilla sugar and lemon juice.

2 Dilute the puréed melon with mineral water or Prosecco. Pour into a tall glass and garnish with mint leaves.

Makes 1 glass. About 85 kcal/360 kJ per glass.
Fat: 0 g • Carbohydrate: 18 g • Protein: 0 g

Blackcurrant and lemon kefir

Blackcurrant juice and kefir: an ideal combination and a perfect way to ward off colds during winter without piling up the calories.

❶ Mix the blackcurrant juice, lemon juice and rosehip pulp together. Add the kefir, stir well and season with a pinch of cinnamon.

Makes 1 glass. About 205 kcal/860 kJ per glass.

Fat: 3 g • Carbohydrate: 26 g • Protein: 10 g

100 ml/3½ fl oz (½ cup) blackcurrant juice

1 tablespoon lemon juice

1 tablespoon rosehip purée

200 ml/7 fl oz (⅞ cup) kefir

1 pinch cinnamon

Beetroot (red beet) and carrot drink

A spicy cocktail, rich in vitamins A and C, seasoned with a little grated horseradish. Carrot juice and beetroot juice are available from health food shops, but they must be unsweetened.

❶ Mix together the beetroot (red beet) juice, carrot juice and sour cream. Stir well and season with freshly ground pepper.

❷ Peel some horseradish, grate finely and add to the mixed juices. Wash the parsley, chop the leaves finely and sprinkle on the juice.

Makes 1 glass. About 120 kcal/505 kJ per glass.

Fat: 1 g • Carbohydrate: 26 g • Protein: 3 g

200 ml/7 fl oz (7/8 cup) beetroot (red beet) juice

200 ml/7 fl oz (7/8 cup) carrot juice

1 teaspoon sour cream

freshly ground pepper

1 small piece horseradish

a few parsley leaves

Green tea drink

Green tea is an excellent thirst quencher and is much healthier than coffee or Indian tea. In Asia, green tea is believed to have medicinal properties such as lowering cholesterol levels.

1 tea bag green tea

1 tea bag peppermint tea

1 teaspoon lime juice

pinch ground ginger

1 teaspoon honey

❶ Bring about 250 ml/8 fl oz (1 cup) water to the boil, remove from the heat and leave to cool a little. Put two tea bags in a pre-heated teapot and pour the hot water on top, allow to draw for about 3 minutes.

❷ Season the green tea with lime juice and ground ginger. Sweeten with honey according to taste.

Makes 1 glass. About 1 kcal/5 kJ per glass.

Fat: 0 g • Carbohydrate: 0 g • Protein: 0 g

Winter punch

You can also make steaming hot punch without fattening ingredients such as alcohol or sugar. This punch consists of an infusion of fragrant herbs with the addition of orange juice.

❶ Heat about 300 ml/10 fl oz (1¼ cups) water in a small saucepan. Add the cloves, cardamom and cinnamon stick. Bring briefly to the boil. Suspend the tea bag in the saucepan, cover and simmer for about 10 minutes over a low heat.

❷ Remove the tea bag, cinnamon stick and cloves from the liquid. Add the orange and lemon juice. Heat the punch but do not boil. Sweeten with honey according to taste and serve hot.

Makes 1 glass. About 80 kcal/330 kJ per glass.
Fat: 0 g • Carbohydrate: 18 g • Protein: 0 g

1 cinnamon stick
3 cloves
1 pinch ground cardamom
1 tea bag mallow tea
juice of 1 orange
juice of 1 lemon
1 teaspoon honey

Cooking glossary

Glossary of technical and foreign language cooking terms

baking, roasting

Cooking food in the oven in a heat-resistant dish, in a baking tin (pan) or on a baking (cookie) sheet. The food is cooked by the hot air of a conventional or a fan oven (in a fan oven the same cooking effect is achieved with a lower temperature; see the maker's manual). The temperature most commonly used is 180°C (350°F), Gas Mark 4, which is ideal for cakes, biscuits (cookies), tarts, flans, roasts, fish and poultry. For puff pastry, soufflés and gratins the temperature should be between 200°C (400°F), Gas mark 6 and 220°C (425°F), Gas mark 7. More delicate food such as fish, veal and some poultry may need a lower heat, from 150°C (300°F), Gas mark 2 to 160°C (325°F), Gas mark 3.

As a rule of thumb, the lower the temperature, the longer the cooking time.

bain-marie

A container of hot water in which or over which food is gently cooked. It may be a rectangular pan in which pans are placed, but in the domestic kitchen it usually takes the form of a double boiler, a saucepan with a smaller pan fitting over it. It can be improvised satisfactorily by using a bowl over a saucepan containing about 2.5 cm/1 inch of hot water.

A bain-marie is used when it is essential not to overheat what is being cooked. It is used for processes such as melting chocolate, and for cooking sauces or puddings containing cream or eggs. For instance, to make a chocolate mousse, the egg whites are beaten stiff over a warm bain-marie. This makes a particularly airy, light yet firm mousse. A bain-marie is also indispensable for making a successful Hollandaise or Béarnaise sauce. The egg yolks are slowly heated while being stirred until they reach the correct consistency, so that they combine with the melted butter whisked into it little by little.

barding

Covering very lean meat such as saddle of venison, pheasant or saddle of hare with slices of bacon, secured with kitchen string. This ensures that the meat remains juicy and does not dry out, while also adding a pleasant flavour to the meat.

basting

Spooning liquid over food while it is being roasted. Normally the cooking juices are used, but butter, wine, stock (broth) or plain water can be used as well. This constant basting and 'looking after' the meat ensures that it remains juicy and does not dry out. The basting liquid acquires a very intense flavour.

beurre manié

Kneaded butter, used to thicken casseroles

and sauces. Equal amounts of flour and butter are kneaded together and added as small knobs into boiling liquid while stirring constantly. This thickening agent has a delicious buttery taste and it is easy to handle because the butter and flour are mixed before being adding to the liquid, reducing the risk of lumps forming in the course of cooking.

blanching

Cooking vegetables such as spinach, leeks and carrots briefly in fast-boiling water. It is important to refresh the vegetables by plunging them in ice-cold water immediately afterwards. This ensures that the vegetables remain crisp and retain their original colour. After blanching, the vegetables are heated in hot stock (broth) or butter before serving.

blini

Pancake (crepe) made of a Russian batter using buckwheat flour, fried in a special small frying pan (skillet) about 15 cm (6 in) in diameter. Wheat flour is often added to the buckwheat flour so that it binds more easily. Blinis are usually served with caviar. They are also delicious with braised meat and game.

boiling

Cooking in liquid that is boiling. The process is synonymous with the concept of cooking. The food is cooked in a large amount of water and the agitation of the liquid will prevent the ingredients sticking to each other. So long as the water is boiling, the temperature will be 100°C (212°F) for the whole of the cooking time.

bouquet garni

A small bundle of various fresh herbs (usually parsley, thyme and bay leaves), tied together and cooked with the food. The bouquet garni is removed before serving.

braising

This refers to a method of cooking which combines frying, simmering and steaming. First the food is seared in hot oil or fat on all sides. This seals the meat, forming a thin crust; this also forms roasting matter on the bottom of the pan which is very important for the colour and flavour of the sauce. Liquid is then added to the meat, the pan is sealed with a lid and the food is slowly braised in a preheated oven. The method is also good for vegetable and fish dishes. It is excellent for less tender, strongly flavoured cuts of meat such as oxtail, goulash, braising steak or stewing lamb.

breadcrumbs

Dried white crumbs, made from stale bread without the crust. They are used in stuffing mixtures or to coat fish, poultry or other meats such as lamb chops.

brunoise

Finely diced vegetables or potatoes.

canapé

Small, bite-sized pieces of bread with various toppings such as smoked salmon, foie gras, caviar, smoked duck breast, ham and so on. They are served as an appetizer.

carcass

The carcass of poultry used in the preparation of chicken stock (broth). Fish bones are used in a similar way to make fish stock (broth).

carving

Cutting meat or poultry into slices or small pieces for serving. It is a good idea to carve on a carving board with a groove for the juices, using a special carving knife.

casserole

A large heat-resistant cooking pot usually made of cast iron or earthenware, excellent for slow-cooked dishes, braises and stews such as oxtail and game ragout. Because of the casserole's large surface area and the lengthy cooking time, the meat is able to release its full flavour. Casseroles may be round or oval, the latter shape being ideally suited for long-shaped pieces of meat such as leg of lamb, rolled cuts of meat or a chicken.

célestine

Fine strips of pancake (crepe) added to soup as a garnish.

chiffonade

Finely cut strips of lettuce, often served with shrimp cocktail.

chinois

Conical strainer or sieve used to strain sauces and soups.

clarification

The removal of cloudy matter from soups, stock (broth) or jelly with lightly beaten egg white. The egg white attracts all the foreign particles which cause the cloudiness and they can then be easily removed. The operation is carried out as follows. A lightly beaten egg white is added to some lean minced (ground) beef and chopped vegetables and a few ice cubes are stirred in. The mixture is added to the stock (broth), which should also be well chilled. Heat up while stirring constantly. The egg white begins to thicken at 70°C (160°F) and in the process it attracts all the impurities in the stock (broth). The stock (broth) becomes clear while developing a very intense flavour, as a result of the beef and vegetables. Fish and vegetable stock (broth) can also be clarified in the same way; in these cases the meat is omitted.

coating

The operation of pouring sauce over vegetables, meat or fish.

It also describes the technique of covering slices of meat and fish with beaten egg and breadcrumbs before frying them in hot oil. This gives the food a crisp coating while keeping the inside moist and juicy.

concassée

Blanched, peeled, quartered and de-seeded tomatoes, finely chopped. The term may also be applied to herbs.

consommé

Simple soup made of meat or chicken stock (broth), sometimes garnished. When clarified, it is known as clear or "double" consommé. Cold consommé is often a jelly.

cream soup, velouté soup

Cream soups are thickened with béchamel sauce. Velouté soups are thickened with an egg and cream mixture. The soup should not be brought back to the boil after the mixture has been added because the egg yolk would curdle.

crepes

Thin pancakes made from a batter consisting of milk, flour and eggs. The pancakes are cooked slowly in a frying pan (skillet) until golden. They can be served as a dessert, plain with a sprinkling of sugar and lemon juice, or spread or filled with jam or chocolate. They can also be served as a savoury dish, stuffed with vegetable or other fillings.

deep-frying

The process of cooking food by immersion in hot fat. When the food is cooked and crisp, it is removed from the fat or oil in its basket or with a skimming ladle and left to drain thoroughly on kitchen paper. Because hot oil or fat often spatters it is vital to be extremely careful and avoid the risk of fire. An electric chip pan with an adjustable thermostatically controlled temperature control is an excellent idea not only because it is safer but it also creates much less of a smell. Peeled potatoes cut into chips (sticks) or slices, shrimps and vegetables in batter are ideal for deep-frying, while deep-fried semolina dumplings are delicious served in soup. Deep-frying is also

used for sweet dishes such as doughnuts and apple fritters.

duxelles

Garnish or stuffing consisting of finely chopped mushrooms sweated with diced onions and herbs.

forcemeat or stuffing

Finely chopped meat or fish used to stuff eggs, meat, pasta and so on. It can make a dish in its own right, as in the case of meat balls and quenelles, for example. It is also used as a basis for terrines and pâtés such as deer terrine or wild boar pâté.

filleting

The operation of cutting off the undercut of beef sirloin or similar cuts of pork (tenderloin), veal or lamb; removing the breasts of poultry from the carcass; or cutting the flesh of fish in strip-like pieces from the backbone.

flambé

Pouring spirits (such as brandy, rum or Grand Marnier) over food and setting light to it. The process is used with both savoury and sweet dishes, such as Crêpes Suzette. The spirits need to be warmed slightly first.

fleurons

Small pieces of puff pastry baked into various shapes such as flowers, little ships or shrimps. They are served with fish dishes in a sauce or with chicken fricassée.

flouring

The coating of pieces of fish or meat with flour before frying. This forms a tasty crust round the meat or fish which will be particularly juicy as a result.

frying

Frying is the process of cooking food in hot fat. The best fats and oils for frying are therefore ones that can be heated to a high temperature such as sunflower oil, clarified butter or goose fat. When butter is used, a little oil is often added to raise the temperature it will reach without burning. Some cuts of meat such as beef steaks or pork cutlets may be fried in a non-stick griddle pan without any fat.

gazpacho

Cold Spanish vegetable soup made with fresh tomatoes, cucumbers, garlic and fresh herbs. It is particularly delicious on a hot summer's day.

glazing

Creating a glossy surface on vegetables, meat, fish or puddings. A suitable stock (broth), the cooking juices, a light caramel, jelly, hot jam or icing is poured over the food in question.

gnocchi

Small dumplings, originally Italian, made from potato, semolina or bread flour, depending on the region, poached briefly in boiling water.

gratiné

Baking dishes under a very high top heat until a brown crust has formed. The ideal topping is grated cheese, breadcrumbs or a mixture of the two.

grilling (broiling)

Cooking with intense radiant heat, provided by gas, electricity or charcoal, the latter giving the food a particularly delicious flavour. The food is cooked on a grid without fat, and grilling (broiling) is therefore particularly good for people who are calorie conscious. Meat, fish, poultry and even vegetables can be cooked in this way.

healthy eating

A well-balanced, varied diet based on wholesome, nutritious foods in the right proportion. Ingredients recommended include wholemeal (wholewheat) products, organic meat, fish and poultry and fresh fruit and vegetables.

julienne

Peeled vegetables cut into thin sticks, the length and thickness of matchsticks. They are cooked in butter or blanched and used as a garnish for soup, fish, meat or poultry dishes.

jus

The name given to cooking juices produced during roasting. It is also used to describe brown stock (broth) prepared from various kinds of meat.

kaltschale

Literally "cold cup", this is a cold sweet soup made with fruit and wine. The fruit, for instance raspberries, melon and strawberries, is finely puréed with lemon juice and wine if so desired to which fresh herbs are added. It is important that it is served chilled.

larding needle

Special needle for pulling lardons (strips of pork fat) through lean meat to keep it moist and make it more tender.

marinade

A mixture based on vinegar, lemon juice, buttermilk or yoghurt, with onions and other vegetables, spices and herbs. Meat or fish is steeped in the mixture for several hours to make it tender and enhance its flavour. Marinades can also be used for dressing salads or for marinating meat that is already tender. Meat marinades give sauces a particularly delicious flavour because they have absorbed the various flavours from the herbs, vegetables and spices.

marinating

Steeping meat or fish in a liquid containing salt, wine, vinegar, lemon juice or milk, and flavourings such as herbs and spices. Marinating has a tenderizing effect on the food and also improves the flavour because of the various ingredients added to the marinade. In addition, marinating also has a preserving effect on meat or fish so that it keeps longer. For instance, raw salmon may be marinated in salt, sugar, herbs and spices.

minestrone

Classic Italian vegetable soup using a wide variety of vegetables, the selection depending on the region and the season. However, pasta and beans are essential ingredients.

mirepoix

Finely diced vegetables, often with the addition of bacon and herbs, fried in butter and used as a basis for sauces.

muffins

Round, flat rolls made with yeast dough and baked. In America, muffins are sweet rolls, using baking powder as a raising agent, made in special muffin pans. There are many varieties made, for instance with blueberries, raspberries, red currants or chocolate.

pie

A sweet or savoury dish baked in a pastry shell with a pastry top. It is made in a pie tin (pan) with a slanting edge 5 cm (2 in) high. The lid of dough should have a small opening in the middle so that the steam can escape, preventing the pie crust from swelling up.

ramekin or cocotte

A small, round oven-proof china or earthenware dish in which individual portions are cooked and served.

reducing

Concentrating a liquid by boiling it so that

the volume is reduced by evaporation. It increases the flavour of what is left. Strongly reducing a sauce gives a particularly tasty result with a beautiful shine.

refreshing

Dipping food, particularly vegetables, briefly in cold water after cooking to preserve the colour, mineral content and vitamins. The cooked vegetables or other items are then drained in a colander.

roasting

See baking.

roux

A mixture of butter and flour used to thicken sauces. The mixture is made by melting butter and stirring in flour. This is then diluted with milk or stock (broth) and cooked for at least 15 minutes while stirring constantly. For a dark roux, the flour is cooked until it turns brown before liquid is added. Because this reduces the thickening quality of the flour, the amount of flour should be increased.

royale

A custard-like cooked egg garnish. Milk and eggs are stirred together, seasoned, poured into small buttered moulds and poached in a bain-marie at 70–80°C (160–180°F). They are then turned out and diced.

salamander

Electric appliance used to caramelize or brown the top of certain dishes. It is comparable to a grill, which is normally used as a substitute.

sauté

Cooking food in fat in a frying pan (skillet). Small, uniform pieces of meat, fish, chopped vegetables or sliced potatoes are cooked in a pan while being tossed to prevent them sticking. In this way all sides of the food are cooked.

simmering

Cooking food in liquid over a low heat, just below boiling point. This method of cooking is often used for making soups and sauces since it makes the food tender and enables it to develop its full aroma.

soufflé

Particularly light, aerated dish made with beaten egg white which may be sweet or savoury. A meal which finishes with a mouth-watering chocolate soufflé will always be remembered with great pleasure.

soup bones

Meat bones, poultry carcass or fish bones used in making stock (broth). These are very important ingredients because they give an intense flavour to the stock (broth). Smooth beef and veal bones are ideal, but the marrow bone has the most flavour. It is important that the bones should be purchased from a reliable butcher and come from a guaranteed source so as to avoid any risk of BSE (mad cow disease).

steaming

Cooking over boiling water so that the food is out of contact with the liquid and cooks in the steam. To achieve this, the food is cooked in a perforated container over lightly boiling water or stock (broth). This method of cooking ensures that vegetables keep their flavour particularly well. They remain crisp and full of taste. Fish too can be cooked in this way without any additional fat but simply with herbs and spices. Steaming is particularly good for the preparation of low-calorie dishes for people who must follow a low-fat diet for reasons of health. But it will also appeal to everyone who loves the pure, genuine flavour of food.

stock (broth)

The flavoured liquid base of soups and sauces. Basic meat stocks (broths) for soups and sauces are made by simmering meat and bones of veal, beef, game, poultry or fish for several hours. As the liquid simmers gently, the constantly forming foam is periodically removed with a skimming ladle. When the stock (broth) has cooled down, the layer of fat can be removed so that the stock (broth) becomes light and clear. Vegetable stock (broth) is made in a similar way by boiling vegetables and herbs

straining

Filtering solid matter from liquids or draining liquids from raw or cooked food. Soups, sauces and stock (broth) are poured or pressed through a fine sieve. In the case of a stock (broth) the sieve may be lined with a coarse cloth.

string

Kitchen string is used to truss poultry or to tie a joint of meat so that it keeps its shape while being cooked.

suprême

Breast of chicken or game. The name refers to the best part of the bird, which is always prepared with the greatest care.

sweating

Frying the food lightly in a little fat in a pan over moderate heat, so that it softens but does not brown.

tartlet

Small tart made from short crust or puff pastry with a sweet or savoury filling.

tenderizing

Making tough meat tender by beating it. The meat is placed between two sheets of foil and beaten with a mallet or the bottom of a small pan until it has become thin. It is used for roulades, veal escalopes and so on.

thickening

The addition of a substance to a sauce or soup to thicken it. There are several common methods. Flour may be added and stirred continuously until the liquid thickens. A variation is to mix butter and flour as a roux to which the liquid is slowly added, again stirring constantly. Alternatively egg yolk or cream can be stirred into the liquid to make an emulsion. On no account must it be allowed to boil or it will curdle. After the yolk has been stirred into the sauce or soup, it must not be cooked any more or it will curdle.

timbale

Mould lined with pastry, blind-baked and filled with meat, fish or other ingredients in a sauce, baked in the oven or cooked in a bain-marie.

trimming

The removal of connective tissue and fat from all kind of meats. The off-cuts are used in the preparation of stock (broth) and sauces. It is important to use a very sharp knife, held flat against the meat so as not to remove too much meat in the process.

turning

Forming vegetables and potatoes into decorative shapes, such as balls, ovals or spirals. This is carried out using a small knife with a crescent-shaped blade.

zest

The thin outer rind of oranges or lemons, used for its flavour and fragrance. It is cut from the pith in thin strips, using a zester.

Herbs and spices

agar

Thickening agent made from dried algae from Asia. It is used as a vegetable gelling agent, for instance, in the manufacturing of blancmange powder, jelly or processed cheese. Agar only dissolves in very hot liquid and has highly gelatinous properties. It is therefore important to follow the instructions very carefully. It is particularly useful in vegetarian cuisine where it is an alternative to gelatine, which is made from beef bones. Agar is often combined with other thickening agents such as carob bean flour because it is very indigestible. This makes it a much more effective thickening agent.

allspice

These brown berries are grown in tropical countries, particularly Jamaica. The complex, multi-layered aroma of allspice is at its best when the fresh grains are crushed in a mortar. It is used to season lamb and beef ragouts, sausages, pies and gingerbread.

aniseed

Aniseed is often associated with the delicious aroma of Christmas cakes and pastries. The seed can be used whole, crushed or ground. It is also used in savoury dishes, for instance in the seasoning and marinades of fish and preparation of fish stock (broth). It is the main flavour of alcoholic drinks such as pastis and ouzo.

basil

Basil is undoubtedly the king of all fresh herbs used in the kitchen. It is an aromatic annual herb that plays an important part in a wide variety of dishes. It has a particular affinity with tomatoes and it is used in salads and many Mediterranean dishes.

basil, Thai

Thai basil is an important herb in Thai cuisine, used in baked noodle dishes, sauces and curries. It is available in many shops specialising in eastern food. It is very delicate and should be used as fresh as possible.

bay leaves

The leathery leaves of the bay tree have a spicy, bitter taste which becomes even stronger when dried. It is one of the ingredients of a bouquet garni. The fresh leaves are added to fish, when dried it is an important ingredient of many preserved dishes, such as braised meat marinated in vinegar and herbs, or pickled gherkins.

borage

A herb with hairy leaves and wonderful blue flowers. It has a slightly bitter, tangy taste reminiscent of cucumber and is mainly used in drinks such as Pimms. It is also a good accompaniment to salads, soups, cabbage and meat dishes.

burnet, salad

The leaves must be harvested before the plant flowers. Salad burnet is used in the same way as borage. It is only used fresh since it loses its aroma completely when dried.

caraway

Caraway is the traditional spice used in rich, fatty dishes such as roast pork, sauerkraut, raw cabbage dishes and stews – not simply for its aromatic flavour but also because of its digestive properties. It is added to some cheeses. Whole or ground, it is also used in spiced bread and cakes. Many liqueurs contain caraway because of its digestive properties.

cardamom

After saffron, cardamom is one of the most expensive spices in the world. Removed from the pod, the seeds are used ground. Just a pinch will be enough to add a delicious taste to rice dishes, cakes or gingerbread.

chervil

The fine flavour of chervil will enhance any spring or summer dish. It can be used in salads, soups and fish dishes and it is also very decorative.

chilli peppers

Red or green chilli peppers are hot and add a spicy, aromatic pungency to food. They are available fresh, dried, ground, pickled or in the form of a paste or essence (extract). When using fresh peppers, it is advisable to remove the seeds which are the hottest part. They are especially popular in Central and south-western America, the West Indies and

Asia, forming an integral part of many dishes originating in these regions.

chives

This is one of the great traditional cooking herbs which is available throughout the year. Very versatile, chives are sold fresh in bunches and are delicious with fromage frais, bread and butter, scrambled eggs or fresh asparagus. The beautiful blue flowers of the chive plant are very decorative and also delicious, making a great addition with the leaves to any salad in the summer.

cloves

The flower buds of the clove tree have an intensely spicy aroma with a bitter, woody taste. That is why it should be used sparingly. Cloves are used in marinades, red cabbage and braised dishes as well as in mulled wine and many Christmas cakes and buns.

coriander (cilantro)

Coriander seeds have been used for a long time, mainly as a pickling spice and in Oriental dishes. Fresh green coriander leaves (cilantro) have become available in many countries much more recently. Finely chopped, this sweetish spicy herb adds an exotic aroma to many dishes, including guacamole. It should be used with discretion by those who are not used to the taste.

cress

The small-leafed relative of the watercress is slightly less aromatic. It is usually sold as small plants in paper containers or as seeds to grow oneself, often with mustard as the mustard and cress used in elegant sandwiches. Cress is commonly used to garnish egg dishes and salads.

cumin

This classic spice is common in eastern cuisine and is a fundamental ingredient of curry powder and curry pastes. It adds an interesting, exotic flavour to braised dishes such as lamb, kid or beef.

curry powder

Curry powder may be made from as many as 30 spices, including among others turmeric, pepper, cumin, caraway, cloves, ginger and allspice. It is extremely versatile and in addition to its use in curries it can be used in small quantities to add flavour to many meat, fish and poultry dishes.

dill

An annual sweetish aromatic herb, common in northern European cooking but seldom used in Mediterranean dishes. The feathery leaves are used fresh in fish dishes, sauces, with fromage frais, and in vegetable dishes. Cucumber pickles (dill pickles) make use of the leaves and the seeds.

fennel

Fennel leaves have a slight flavour of aniseed and are commonly used with fish. The seeds are sometimes used to season bread. When added to fish dishes and fish stock (broth), the seeds are crushed first.

fines herbes

Classic French combination of herbs, made from parsley, tarragon, chervil, chives, and perhaps thyme, rosemary and other herbs. Fines herbes may be used fresh, dried or frozen. The commonest use is in omelettes.

galangal

A close relative of the ginger family which is much used in south-eastern cuisine. The roots can used fresh, dried, ground or dried.

garam masala

The meaning of this Indian name is 'hot mixture', and it consists of up to 13 spices. It plays an important part in the cooking of India, where it is home-made, so that its composition varies from family to family. Garam masala is available commercially in supermarkets and in shops specialising in Asian food.

garlic

Cooking without garlic is unimaginable to anyone who loves and enjoys the pleasures of the Mediterranean. Freshly chopped, it enhances salads and cold sauces, roasts, stews, braised and grilled (broiled) dishes, all benefit from the addition of garlic. Another popular use is in garlic bread.

gelatine

Gelatine is a thickening agent made from beef bones. Leaf gelatine must be soaked thoroughly in plenty of cold water for five or ten minutes before using it. It is then squeezed well and diluted in warm water. A special technique is needed when using gelatine in cream-based dishes. A few spoonfuls of cream are stirred into the gelatine. This mixture is then stirred into the rest of the cream. In this way lumps will be avoided.

ginger

The juicy roots of ginger have a sharp fruity aroma. Ginger adds an interesting, exotic touch to both savoury and sweet dishes. Because ginger freezes very well it can be kept for a long time without losing any of its flavour. A piece can be broken off whenever it is needed.

lavender

The taste of lavender is bitter and spicy. It can be used as a seasoning for lamb-based dishes, meat and fish stews and salads. The flowers are particularly decorative.

lovage

Lovage has a celery-like taste and both the stems and the leaves can be used in soup, salads and sauces. The finely chopped leaves are sometimes added to bread dumplings, and to the stuffing for breast of veal to which it adds a particularly delicate flavour.

marjoram

Sweet marjoram is a popular herb with a distinctive aroma. It can be used either fresh and dried, but like almost all herbs it is best when it is fresh. Marjoram is delicious in potato soups and omelettes. Pot marjoram is

a hardier form with a stronger flavour, so it is advisable not to use too much.

mint

Mint is delicious as mint tea and also in puddings such a mint ice cream, and in drinks. It is part of many soups, salads and meat dishes, and is often added to potatoes and peas. Mint sauce is served with lamb. Mint leaves are also often used as decoration.

mugwort

This is a variety of wormwood. It grows in the wild and the sprigs should be collected just before the plants flower. They can also be dried for later use. Mugwort is popular with roast goose and game.

mustard seeds

Mustard seeds are one of the most important ingredients in pickled vegetables such as gherkins, courgettes (zucchini), pumpkin, mixed pickles and pickled cocktail onions. They are often used too in braised beef, marinated in vinegar and herbs.

nasturtiums

Nasturtium flowers are very decorative and the leaves are delicious, their sharp, peppery taste adding a spicy touch to any salad.

nutmeg

Grated nutmeg is delicious in soups, stews, potato purée and cabbage. It is a also a traditional seasoning in Christmas cakes and confectionery. It tastes best when freshly grated.

oregano

Also known as wild marjoram, oregano is much used in Italian cuisine. It is essential in many dishes such as pizzas, pasta with tomato sauce and aubergine (egg plant) dishes. In the case of pizzas it is best to use dried oregano because the fresh leaves become brown in the very strong heat of the hot oven, thus losing much of their flavour.

parsley

The most popular of all herbs, two varieties are common, one with curly leaves and the other with smooth leaves. But it is not only the leaves that are used; the roots too are full of flavour and are delicious added to soups and sauces. Parsley has a deliciously fresh aroma and a strong taste. It is also extremely rich in vitamins and minerals, so it is an important herb for use in winter.

pepper

Black pepper and white pepper have different tastes as well as looking different. Black pepper is obtained by harvesting the unripe fruit, while white pepper is the ripe fruit which is peeled before being dried. White pepper is milder, more delicate in taste and not as sharp as black.

purslane

The green, fleshy leaves can be used raw in salads or used as a vegetable in its own right

as in the Far East. The delicious leaves have a slightly salty flavour.

rosemary

Rosemary has a particular affinity with lamb, which is often roasted with a few sprigs. It is particularly popular in France where it is used in many dishes such as soups, potatoes, vegetables, meat and fish dishes. Dried, chopped rosemary is one of the ingredients of *herbes de Provence*.

saffron

This bright orange spice is the 'golden' condiment of good cuisine, providing an inimitable flavour and colour. It consists of the dried stigmas of the saffron crocus, and about 4,000 of these are needed for 25 g (1 oz), which accounts for its high cost. But only a small amount is needed; just a few filaments or a tiny pinch of ground saffron will be enough to add a very special taste to bouillabaisse, paella or risotto.

sage

The sharp, slightly bitter taste of sage is ideal with roast goose or roast lamb. Often used in sausages, it is also one of the most important ingredients of the Italian classic 'Saltimbocca' (veal escalope with sage and Parma ham). The fresh leaves are delicious dipped in batter and fried.

savory

Savory is a peppery herb used in many bean-based dishes and also in stews and casseroles. The stem is cooked in the stew while the young shoots are chopped up and added to the dish just before the end of the cooking time.

star anise

This is the small star-shaped seed of the Chinese aniseed, native to China. The flavour is a little more bitter than aniseed itself. It can be used for baking and cooking and adds a delicious flavour to leg of lamb and dried apricots or in sweet and sour beef stew. It can also be used in puddings such as apple or quince compote.

tamarind

The pods contains a very sour juice which is much used in Indian and Thai cooking. Dishes such as baked fish with tamarind sauce, cherry tomatoes and fresh ginger are quite delicious.

tarragon

Tarragon has a delicate, spicy flavour. It can be used on its own as in tarragon vinegar or tarragon mustard, in Béarnaise as well as in a wide range of poultry and fish dishes. It is also excellent when combined with other herbs such as chervil, chives and parsley. The variety to be used is French tarragon. Russian tarragon grows easily from seed but has little flavour.

thyme

Like rosemary, this sweetish spicy herb is particularly good with Mediterranean food. It is an essential part of a bouquet garni and one of the main ingredients of *herbes de Provence*. Thyme will add a special touch to any dish, whether meat, fish, poultry or vegetables.

turmeric

Turmeric is much used in oriental cuisine. It is one of the basic ingredients of curry powder, Thai fish and meat curries and Indian rice dishes. It has an intense, yellow colour, but it should not be confused with saffron which has a very different taste.

vanilla

The fruit pods (beans) of the tropical vanilla orchid tree add a delicious aroma to cakes, puddings, ice cream, confectionery and so on. In cakes it is best to use vanilla essence (extract) while to make ice-cream and rice pudding, the crushed pod (bean) is added to the hot liquid so that it releases its delicate aroma. Vanilla sugar is made by leaving a pod (bean) in a container of sugar.

wasabi

Very sharp green radish usually available as a paste or powder. It is used to season sushi and many other Japanese dishes. It is important not to add too much. Wasabi is usually served separately as well so that every one can mix it to the sharpness they like.

watercress

Watercress grows in the wild but it should not be eaten in case it contains parasites. Cultivated watercress is readily available. This is grown in watercress beds with pure water of the correct temperature running through them. Watercress has a hot, spicy taste and is delicious on its own, on bread and butter, in green salads, in cream soups, in risottos and in potato salad.

woodruff, sweet

Smelling of new-mown hay, sweet woodruff is only available in May, and it is therefore best-known as the essential ingredient in the aromatic drinks of traditional Maytime celebrations, such as the May wine cup in Germany and May wine punch in the United States. It is delicious in desserts, such as fresh strawberries marinated in woodruff, or wine jelly with fruit and fresh woodruff.

Index

List of recipes

Recipes by category

Breakfast

Snacks between meals

Concept and execution:
twin books, Munich
Editorial: Gisela Witt, Dagmar Fronius-Gaier, Juliane von Akerman, Simone Steger
Layout and typesetting: HUBERT Medien Design, Munich
Photography: Brigitte Sporrer, Alena Hrbkova
Food styling: Hans Gerlach, Christine Kranzfelder
Cover design: BOROS, Wuppertal
© cover photograph: Stockfood/Caggiano Photography
Printing: Druckerei Appl, Wemding

© 2001 DuMont Buchverlag, Köln (monte von DuMont)
All rights reserved

ISBN 3-7701-7029-6

Printed in Germany

The recipes in this book have been carefully researched and worked out. However, neither the authors nor the publishers can be held liable for the contents of this book.

Picture acknowledgments:
The editors and publishers thank the following for their help in the creation of this book:

Glashaus, Munich: 129,149,152,157,170,175,178,185
Küche und Bar, Munich: 81

The Author:
Sandra Schäffer lives and works in Taunus, Germany. She is a qualified cook and home economist. She is also a consultant dietician in a health clinic and has published several nutritional guides.

The photographers:
Brigitte Sporrer and Alena Hrbkova met each other while training as photographers in Munich, Germany. After working as assistants to various advertising and food photographers, they now each have their own studios in Munich and Prague respectively.

The food stylists:
Hans Gerlach is a skilled cook and architect from Munich, who also works as a freelance food stylist. His clients include print and TV advertising production companies, and he also contributes his skills to cookery books.

Christine Kranzfelder, a qualified cook, lives and works in Augsburg. She works for the "food&text" agency, specialising in cookery books, but she is also involved in advertising production.

DUMONT monte

Already published

ISBN 3-7701-7001-6

ISBN 3-7701-7004-0

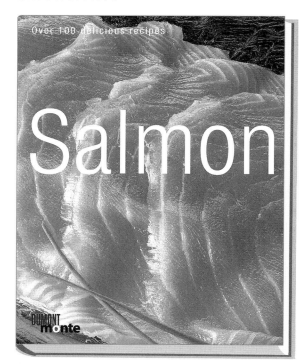

ISBN 3-7701-7002-4
(not available in USA and Canada)

Each title:
160 pages
100 colour photographs
230 x 280 mm / 9 x 11 inches
hardcover, £ 9.99 / $ 14.95

☞ **Over 100 classic and creative
   new recipes**
☞ **Brilliant value – a great gift buy**
☞ **Easy-to-follow methods**
☞ **100 inspirational photographs**

DUMONT monte

Already published

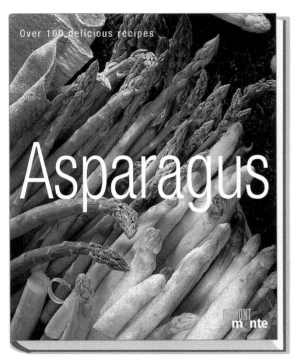

ISBN 3-7701-7046-6

ISBN 3-7701-7029-6

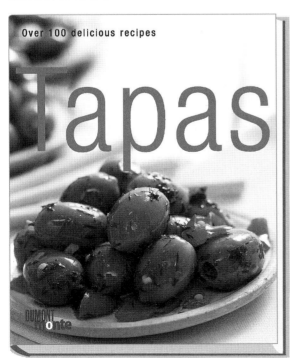

ISBN 3-7701-7003-2

Asparagus
c. 150 pages
over 100 colour photographs
230 x 280 mm / 9 x 11 inches
hardcover, £ 9.99 / $ 15.95

Low Fat
216 pages
over 120 colour photographs
230 x 270 mm / 9 x 11 inches
hardcover, £ 9.99 / $ 17.95

Tapas
164 pages
100 colour photographs
230 x 280 mm / 9 x 11 inches
hardcover, £ 9.99 / $ 14.95